Personal
Recollections

of the

War of 1861

DATE DUE

7 8 2017		

GAYLORD PRINTED IN U.S.A.

Personal Recollections

of the

War of 1861

Charles A. Fuller

Foreword by
Gregory A. Coco

"After Gettysburg" by
Herb S. Crumb

A Reprint by

Edmonston Publishing, Inc.
Hamilton, New York

Personal Recollections is reprinted from a copy in the Colgate University Library, Hamilton, NY.

Library of Congress Catalog Card Number: 89-82533

ISBN 0-9622393-1-3

Printed in the United States of America

10 9 8 7 6 5 4 3 2

Cover design by Ellen Peletz

Contents

Foreword

Nearly ten years have passed since I first had the pleasure of discovering a copy of Charles Fuller's *Personal Recollections of the War of 1861*. It was wedged tightly between two handsome hardcover books on a library shelf where the few overhead lights and two small windows provided the barest illumination for anyone scanning the dusty shelves. The tattered little volume with its simple paper cover immediately intrigued me and I carried it into a secluded alcove where an hour quickly disappeared as I browsed slowly over the hundred or so pages which, even then, were already nearly 75 years old. In the knowledge that I had found an historical treasure, I returned several weeks later to spend the five dollars or so it cost to have it photocopied. It was then placed among my files where it was often referred to and where it remains today. This decision to reproduce Fuller's *Recollections* proved to be a good one, because I was never able to find and purchase the original publication.

The diminutive volume you are now holding has finally brought an end to this dilemma. With the reprinting of Charles Fuller's book a whole new generation now has the opportunity to read and enjoy this unadorned but authentic Civil War classic. Over the years to come, all who purchase it will surely have reason to thank Herb Crumb and the Norwich Civil War Round Table as well as Edmonston Publishing for their efforts to perpetuate the memory and deeds of one of Sherburne's esteemed citizens and veterans, Lieutenant Charles A. Fuller.

The people of Chenango County can be justly proud of men like Charlie Fuller. He and similar ancestors became a part of one of the numerous excellent infantry regiments fielded by New York during the Civil War. The 61st was initially organized in New York City between July and November of 1861 under Colonel Spencer W. Cone, who consolidated the strengths of two early militia units, the Astor Rifles and the Clinton Guards. Many of the maiden volunteers came from New York

City, Albany, and various counties in the state, whereas Fuller's Company "C" was composed primarily of students from Madison University (now Colgate University), and from villages like Hamilton and Sherburne.

By the war's end, the 61st had served approximately four full years, with enlistments and conscripts totalling 1526 men. Of these, 12.6 percent were either killed or mortally wounded; that is, 16 officers and 177 enlisted men. Their battle record was both hazardous and impressive, with participation in at least 44 actions against Confederate forces, 22 of which were important engagements beginning at Fair Oaks in 1862 and ending at Farmville in 1865. Its greatest loss occurred in that first battle, where those raw recruits suffered 110 casualties. And sadly, a fact bemoaned by Fuller throughout his recollections was the pitiful depletion of the line companies as the war progressed. Even as early as the Seven Days' Battles, the enrollment of the 61st had fallen below 420 men. A month later there were approximately 150 men remaining, and by the time of Gettysburg, only 93 officers and enlisted men were present when its threadbare ranks met repeated Southern attacks in the tangled and trampled grain of John Rose's wheatfield.

Fuller recalled one of his most painful memories in a letter written to his family a month after Antietam when he noted that his company could muster only 11 members, and many of these were slightly wounded, sick, paroled prisoners, or in some way "broken in mind and body." His regiment, which officially should have contained 1000 bodies, in Charlie's words, consisted of merely "50 or 60 charter members."

These were sad times, and all occurring within an organization which could securely boast that it was commanded by two of the best colonels in the Union army, Francis Barlow and Nelson Miles.

But Fuller's story is really not about the regiment or its functionary actions between 1861 and 1865. Therefore, if you have purchased this book as a "regimental history" of the 61st (for it, unfortunately, has none) or if you expected these pages to be filled with great and wonderful battle strategy, or the electrifying tactics of famous generals, you will be readily disappointed. For as Fuller states in his recollections: "All this is very tame and personal, and, in many ways, I know can be of but small interest. . . . The reality of war is largely obscured . . . [which] leaves out of sight the fellows stretched out with holes through them or with legs and arms off."

To many of us, of course, this is precisely why we will read his book. The "obscure" is the strength of the personal narrative and makes these stories still very popular to so many readers even a century and a quarter later. We need the mundane, the trivial, as well as the individual horror and brutality brought forth and remembered by the common soldier, the infantryman, the "grunt." These spectacles fascinate those who have not had to actually encounter them, and bring into mind the secret thought that "Yes, it's all exciting and fine, but thank God I didn't have to live it."

Frankly, I like Lieutenant Fuller's recollections just as they are. They are what I, as a veteran, would choose to write. In actuality, the only weak points of the book (and they are brief and few) are the interludes where Fuller quotes from contemporary printed sources to expound upon the performance of his regiment in a particular situation or to defend it in some way. These flattering excerpts can naturally be expected, as he rightfully felt good about his old unit. However, Fuller chiefly remains true to his intention of voicing only the interesting experiences he was actually a part of.

This theme abounds in examples such as the time Charlie moved into a battle line during the night, nerves all amuck, hearing what he believed to be the cries of horribly wounded men, only to discover the next day that the noise was simply the braying of a collection of commissary mules.

Or he tells of the grotesque sight of a friend whose eyeballs were literally shot out of his head and were seen hanging down on his face, yet the man remained standing in formation.

Other stories were of Colonel Barlow violently punching and beating a coward he discovered running away; the unfamiliar jabber of a "German" regiment going into action; an unusually good description of sick call; comments on his rifled musket; the duties of file closers in battle; the adverse effect of constant hardships on the rank and file; the comical sight of an Irishman who lost his pants during the Battle of Antietam; and the revolting spectacle of a soldier set afire by a shell going through his body with the corpse still smoldering at Charlie's feet.

Scenes like these are infinite and stock this book like the well-filled shelves of a Victorian era pantry. But by far the principal substance of Fuller's recollections is the narrative of his ghastly wounding at Gettysburg and the subsequent adventures he experienced until reaching his home. His powers of description and eye for detail reach a pinnacle during the last 20 pages of the memoir. As a matter of fact, after reading through more than a thousand sources for a book recently published on the field hospitals at Gettysburg, I easily rated Fuller's record as one of the top ten best reminiscences of a wounded man in any battle of the Civil War. It is tragic and poignant, yet a perfect end to a superb account by one participant in that unfortunate war.

A songwriter once said, "War has shattered many young men's dreams, made them disabled, bitter and mean. . . ."

Yet somehow, someway, Charles Fuller appeared to have swallowed his bitter pill better than most. At such a young age, he was reduced to living life as a cripple in a land overflowing with broken bodies and hearts. It was by no means an easy fate. This notion may not readily occur to the reader, as Charlie seems to harbor no anger or resentment. But lest we forget, being strapped through years and years of one's existence with a shattered, useless arm and a leg amputated above the knee could cause many silent tears, moments of quiet rage and unanswered questions as the ex-soldier considers his purpose in the mysterious scheme of things.

It is very likely that by the time Fuller put together his remembrances in the early 1900s, he had actually come to grips with his fate. Forty years is a long time (it's half of the average lifespan), and together with this lengthy respite and the ennobled fact that the restored Union expected her sons to be heroes, it became easier to move ahead.

Charlie Fuller was obviously proud of his service; he had risen from private to lieutenant in a tough, battle-hardened regiment; he was a wounded veteran of a popular war; and he had survived! Fuller simply used the good to conquer the bad. His standing in a small, close-knit community enabled him to overcome the nightmares, the pain, and the enduring handicap, and he did it well, both with grace and honor. And as his peers, family, and neighbors showered him with love and exalted in him, then he in turn took pride in himself, his deeds, even his misfortune. These reminiscences attest to this, as you shall shortly witness.

I do not doubt that you will enjoy reading the forthcoming pages. And in the years to come when your eye catches a glimpse of this little book on your library shelf, your memories of it, like mine, will be fond ones.

Bendersville, PA   Gregory A. Coco
January 1990

Charles A. Fuller
Late of the 61st N.Y.V. Inf.

Personal Recollections

—OF THE—

✖ War of 1861 ✖

as Private, Sergeant and Lieutenant in the Sixty-First Regiment, **New** York Volunteer Infantry by

CHARLES A. FULLER

Prepared from data found in letters, written at the time from the field to the people at home.

NEWS JOB PRINTING HOUSE, SHERBURNE, N. Y.
1906

PERSONAL RECOLLECTIONS

March 1st, 1861, I started for Cleveland, Ohio, to enter the law office of Boardman & Ingersoll as a law student. I was in that city at the time of the inauguration of President Lincoln.

After Sumpter was fired on I was anxious to enlist and go to the front with the "Cleveland Grays," but trouble with my eyes induced me to postpone my enlistment. After the President issued his call for 300,000 additional troops, I learned that Lieut. K. Oscar Broady, a recent graduate of Madison University, who had seen some military service in Sweden, his native country, was raising a Company for the War, in which many Hamilton and Sherburne men were enrolled. Isaac Plumb, one of my most-thought-of friends, was in the number; there were others—Edgar Willey, Isreal O Foote, Fred Ames, and more whose names I do not now recall. I decided to wait no longer, but seek the enemy with the men of this Company.

I left Cleveland Sept. 5th, 1861, and reached Utica Saturday afternoon in time to find that the stage down the valley had gone, and I must remain there until Monday morning, or use some other means of locomotion southward to Sherburne. The question I asked myself was, "Why not test your leg gear NOW, and see what you can do as a foot-man?" I answered "All right." and started out, though it was well into the afternoon. That evening I reached Oriskany Falls, a distance of about 20 miles. I camped for the night at the hotel, but was up the next morning before the hotel people. I left the price of the lodging on the bar, and started south.

It was about 24 miles to Sherburne, which I reached about noon. I supplied the commissary department from houses along the road.

My father and mother had no hint that I had left Cleveland. When I entered the house my mother said, "Why, Charlie Fuller, you've come home to go to war." She was the daughter of a man who was in the Revolutionary Army when but sixteen years of age, and she had always been proud of the fact, and she was, I am sure, gratified that she had a boy desirous of imitating the example of her deceased father.

On my way through Hamiltom, I had left word what I was there for, and I was assured that Lieut. Coultis would soon be down to enroll me.

The next day he was on hand; he had, I believe, been in a militia company; at all events, he appeared in the toggery of a militia officer. He said he was authorized and prepared to "swear me in." I told him I was ready for business, and then and there took the oath. I tried to feel easy and appear unconcerned (whether or not I succeeded to outward appearance I can not say) but I know that inside there was more or less of a lump to swallow, for, to some extent, I realized that it was *not* a picnic.

I was home for a week, in which time four men joined me. They were Lewis R. Foote, Porter E. Whitney, Newel Hill and Albert H. Simmons. To show what war does, the following summary is a fair sample--Foote, wounded at Fair Oaks, discharged; Whitney, several times wounded, lastly in the Wilderness Campaign, 1864, transferred to the Veteran Reserve Corps; Hill, discharged early for physical disability; Simmons, detailed to Commissary Dept., discharged on account of physical disability; Fuller, discharged on account of wounds.

Monday, Sept. 16th, 1861, our squad of five left Sherburne for Hamilton. We were there until Thursday, when we started for Staten Island, the headquarters of the forming regiment. Coultis had about thirty men. We reached the rendezvous about 11 o'clock Friday and received a warm welcome from old friends on the ground.

This forming regiment was located on ground within the present enclosure of Fort Wadsworth, Staten Island. Spencer W. Cone had the Colonel's Commission, and his regiment had the fancy name of "Clinton Guards," whether in honor of George, or DeWitt, I do not know, and perhaps Cone didn't.

The explanation of Broady's connection with Cone's regiment, undoubtedly, is this: The father of Spencer W. Cone was a Baptist Doctor of Divinity, of Baltimore, Md. Probably he was known to, and a friend of the managers of Madison University. Quite likely it was assumed that so good a man as Cone, D. D., would have a son of ability and piety, well calculated to lead his men to victory. or, if to death, the death of the righteous; and, so, I assume, it was regarded as a fortunate circumstance that the young men who had been connected with Madison University were to go into this man's regiment.

Mr. Cone was one of those (what Simeon Cameron is alleged to have characterized a writer) "damned literary fellers." He had been a contributor to the New York Mercury, and other periodicals. He had a penetrating and quite powerful voice, and displayed in his person some of the pomp and circumstance of war, and, to the novices in his camp, he was for a time regarded as a "big injun." Events proved this to be unfounded and, before the regiment really met the enemy, he ceased to be the Colonel. At this time one Manning wore the uniform of Lieutenant-Colonel, and one Lynch that of Major.

A quarrel was worked up among the officers, and, it was said, that Cone proposed to leave it to the line officers whether he should continue as Colonel, or step aside for another. The vote was taken and Cone was loser. Then he refused to abide by the result. He was ordered to leave camp and refused. Hands were laid on him to compel his withdrawal, he resisted with oaths and froth and a show of fight; but he was overcome by superior force and exported from the camp. I think Maj. Lynch assumed command. After a few days the camp was moved a number of miles to a place, called Silver Lake. This move was on Saturday.

The next morning some of the officers were informed that Cone was on the road to this new camp with authority to take command and to place in arrest all of the officers who had aided in his displacement. There was a great scampering on the part of these officers, and soon they were conspicuous by their absence. In a little while the valiant Cone appeared on the color line, and ordered the men to turn out; his order was obeyed. Then he showed authority for taking command of the regiment, and he offered to pardon all who had been in the movement against him, if they would return and promise to be good in the future. The skedadling officers got the word, came back, were forgiven, and resumed their places; that was the last the regiment knew of Manning and Lynch.

The Monday following the regiment moved back to its old quarters near the fort, and remained there till ordered to Washington. In this unfortunate fiasco the regiment lost about two hundred men by desertion, from which depletion it never recovered. When ordered to the seat of war, I think there were not much above 700 men, and the regiment never saw the time when it had full ranks—that fact alone accounts for its not being in the list of those that lost two hundred in battle. I believe the number killed in action, or who died in a short time from battle wounds, was 193, or seven short of the number. When brigaded, my recollection is, that it was at least one hundred and fifty men short of the number of any other regiment. It had the same number of officers that the other regiments had, and, with them, the loss in killed equalled, I believe, the losses in the 5th New Hampshire, which has the distinction of having lost the most men killed in action of any infantry regiment on the Union side in the War of the Rebellion.

Francis C. Barlow was appointed Lieut-Col. in place of Manning, and Capt. Massett was promoted to Major. In each case a good exchange. Barlow did not appear for duty at Staten Island and was not generally known to the regiment until it went into Camp at Kendall Green in Washington, D, C.

Saturday, Nov, 9th, 1861, orders were issued to break camp. The men's knapsacks were loaded down with things necessary and things that *could* be dispensed with, (which were thrown away when real campaigning was entered upon.)

No doubt an average knapsack at this time would weigh from twenty-five pounds and upwards. The regiment left its formation camp for the front about seven hundred strong. We took a steamer and landed at Perth Amboy. There we took cars for Washington, reaching Philadelphia during the night, and were at once marched to a citizens lunch barracks, where the regiment at one time was substantially fed. From an early date in the War the patriotic citizens of Philadelphia did this to every regiment that passed through the city. New York and Philadelphia differ in many ways. In 1861, and during the following years of the War, there was an antipodal difference between these cities in their regard for and treatment of the Union Soldiers. In Philadelphia the troops were, in going out, you might almost say; banqueted, and when the wounded began to come back from the front great hospitals were run by the voluntary services of the best women in the city. I had personal experience in each of these ways showing appreciation of the work of the soldier. I have never heard anyone accuse New Yorkers of making any systematic effort to cheer the boys on as they went out, or care for them as they came back wrecked by disease or torn by the missiles of the enemy. The city of New York is entirely too practical to be diverted by patriotic sentiment, if, as a municipality, it has any.

About 8 a. m., Sunday, we left the city of Brotherly Love and reached Washington at 9 p. m. The regiment was marched into a large building capable of housing a thousand men, called the "Soldiers' Rest," located at the terminus of the Baltimore & Ohio R. R. Monday, Nov. 11th, the regiment was marched into an open field not far from the Capitol and to the right of it as the city is entered, This field was called Kendall Green. For years it has been solidly built upon.

Lieut.-Col. Barlow in this camp first made himself known to the regiment. He was not at first sight an impressive looking officer. He was of medium height, of slight build, with a pallid countenance, and a weakish drawling voice. In his movements there was an appearance of loose jointedness and an absence of prim stiffness. At once schools and drills

were established for commissioned and non-commissioned
officers and rumor credited Barlow with their establishment.
Discipline became stricter: the duties of the soldier were better explained, and the men sensibly improved. There was
no doubt to whom is due the credit for the change. In a
short time there was a feeling in the air that the strength of
the regiment lay in the person of the Lieut.-Colonel. Francis
C. Barlow was a great soldier. He was, in my judgment,
fully equal for a corps commander. He knew the details of
his business; he had the military instinct; and he was fear-
less. At first, from his exacting requirements and severity
he was quite disliked, if not well hated; but, as time went
on, and it was seen that he knew more than any other man,
or set of men, in the regiment—that he knew how to work
his men to the best advantage, and would see that they had
what the regulations prescribed, and, that, when danger was
at hand, he was at the head *leading* them, this animosity
was turned into confidence and admiration.

Thursday, Nov. 28th, the regiment broke camp at Kendall
Green and started with overloaded knapsacks for Alexandria, by the road, some eight or ten miles distant. The
Potomac was crossed on Long Bridge, the road ran by the
partly built Washington Monument. The march was a hard
one, largely on account of the men being loaded like pack
peddlers.

At Alexandria the regiment took cars and was run out a
distance of six or seven miles on the Orange & Alexandria
railroad to a point called Springfield Station. This was a
place consisting of an old wood-colored house. The men
were ordered out, and, as the tents were not expected up
that night, preparations were at once begun to make brush
huts for bivouacing. Some time had been spent, and the
work nearly done when the long roll began to beat. The
men at once took their places behind their stacked arms.
Col. Cone was rushing about in a highly excited manner,
holding a revolver in one hand and his bridle reins in the
other, resolved, no doubt, to die bravely, if need be. There
was not a round of ammunition in the regiment. I never
learned that there was a show of the enemy. Perhaps it

became known at headquarters that we had no loading for our guns. At all events, a train was sent out to take us back to Alexandria. We got back without accident, and spent the night in the round house.

The next day we marched out on the turnpike running near the railroad about three miles, and made a camp called Camp Calfornia. It was at the foot of the hill on which Ft. Worth was built. If I am not mistaken, our regiment, which had been numbered the 61st, was the first one on the ground of the brigade that was to be here formed. In a short time the others arrived and were as follows : 5th New Hampshire, 4th Rhode Island, 81st Pennsylvania, each of them having a larger membership than ours. Brigade General O. O. Howard was assigned to the brigade, which was No. 1 in Sumner's Division. Corps were not yet formed.

Besides guard mountings and dress parades, five or six hours a day were consumed in company, regimental and brigade drills. The men were worked hard, and, by this time it was generally understood that learning to be a soldier was no loafing business.

The first time we saw Nelson A. Miles was in this camp. He then was a fine looking young man on the staff of Gen. Howard.

As the Fall weather came on the men generally took colds that were of the coughing kind; the full strength of cough music was heard at night, when other sounds were hushed. Then, seemingly, every man tuned it up with his own peculiar sort and tone of cough. The concert surpassed in volume that coming from a large frog swamp in the flush of the season. Many became down sick and were sent to hospital. Those who stood the exposure gradually toughened and became proof against such sickness.

One night after tattoo the long roll began to beat. Officers and men hurriedly dressed, snatched their arms and accoutrements and formed in the company streets. As soon as a company was ready it started for the color line, and, as soon as the regiment was formed, it started on a brisk walk towards the front, or in the direction of our pickets. When once fairly under way the order was to "step out," and finally, to "double quick." We went in the direction of Edson's Hill, where our picket reserves were stationed. It was a distance of several miles and was travelled in a short time. It proved to be a sham alarm, and was got up to see how we would perform if it were a genuine affair. For one, I made that midnight march expecting to meet the enemy.

As we were going up the hill where the camp fire of the picket reserves were burning, I heard what I took to be a powerful human groan; I said to myself "this, indeed, is bloody, brutal war," and I was, as best I could, nerving myself to face the enemy and do my duty in the deadly fray. We reached the top of the hill in safety, and there, sitting and sprawling around their camp fires, were our men wholly unconcerned. I determined to know what there was concerning the wounded man whose groan I had heard and I went back where I had heard the sound of pain and found a six-mule team. In going by it had been unobserved. I concluded on this discovery that the outcry of my wounded man was nothing more than the grunting and braying of an ass, and I was relieved.

About the first of January, 1862, orders were isssued for the detail of recruiting parties from every regiment to go to the States for the purpose of getting new men to make good the losses in the field. For this purpose, from the 61st N. Y., Lieut. Wm. H. McIntyre of Co. C was named to command the party. With him were Lieut. Blowers, Co. F, Corporal Jenks and myself of Co. C, and two or three other men whose names I have forgotten. We left camp Monday, Jan. 21st, 1862. We reported to Maj. Sprague, U. S. A., at Albany. He granted us a few days furlough and we all visited our homes.

Our recruiting headquarters were at, or near, 480 Broadway, New York. No bounties were offered, and, while we all did our best, the result was nearly a failure. Not more than a dozen good men were secured. Our party was heartily sick of the job and sincerely desired to be returned to the regiment.

About the 1st of April a movement was made by the Army of the Potomac. At this time army corps had been formed. I think Sumner's, the Second Corps, had but two divisions. The First, Richardson's in which was Howard's brigade; Meagher's, or the Irish brigade, and French's; the Second was commanded by Sedgwick. I believe the corps, division and brigade commanders were as good as any in the army of the Potomac. The first move of the army was on to Centerville, and the Bull Run battlefield. The enemy fell back. Then McClellan changed his base to the peninsula between the York and James rivers.

April 15th, 1862, the recruiting office was closed and our party started for the regiment. We stopped at Fortress Monroe and procured rations. From there took a steamer up the river about 20 miles to Shipping Point. We found our regiment some miles further to the front.

When we reached camp we received a soldier's welcome from the boys. They showed what a few weeks of exposure would do for the outside of a man; skin and clothes; they were tanned, ragged and lousy.

As we were back from the entrenchments some distance, our efforts were mainly directed to building corduroy roads.

Sunday, May 4th, orders came to pack and be ready to move at once. Soon it was reported that Yorktown had been evacuated. We did not get into motion, finally, until the 5th, and then went out but a short distance, when a halt was made until about dark when we again started and went through the rebel defenses. It had rained some during the day and this Virginia mud was a difficult thing to stand on, especially if the standing was on an incline. A slow and laborious march was continued until midnight, or past. When we halted many of the men had fallen out on the march, but came up in the morning. After breakfast a short distance was made; then a halt was ordered; then came the news that Williamsburg had been taken, and the enemy were retreating up the peninsula. The Second Corps, or our division of it, returned to Yorktown and went into camp the next day, which was Wednesday. We remained in this camp until the next Sunday, when we took transports up the York river to West Point, at which place we unshipped Monday, May 12th, and went into camp. I remember that this locality was pleasanter than the country about Shipping Point and in front of Yorktown.

A division of our men had a brush with the enemy here a few days before our arrival. Quite a number of our men were so sick at this place that they were sent back to York-town, and one, at least, of the number died. I refer to Charles Smith, a genial, good man.

Thursday, May 15th, reveille beat at 2 a. m., and we marched at 4 a. m. At first it was fine marching, but to-wards noon a drenching rain set in, and in a short time we were wet to the skin. We made fourteen miles. We went into camp in a piece of woods. While here quite a number of the men were taken with a sudden dizziness, and would fall while drilling. The first orderly of my company was William H. Spencer. He was promoted to First Lieutenant of Deming's Company, and later on to the Captaincy of Brooks's Company. His promotion advanced my best friend, Isaac Plumb, Jr., to first sergeant. For some weeks he had been suffering from a low fever, and Arthur Haskell was acting orderly. In this camp he was taken with this strange dis-ease and sent back, and I was made acting orderly, in which office I acted until after the battle of Fair Oaks.

Sunday, the 18th, we again started and marched five miles and went into camp. By this time the men had become somewhat familiar with Gen I. B. Richardson, their division commander. He was a large, heavy, powerful man, a West Pointer, and commanded, I think, the Second Michigan at Bull Run. He put on no military style : generally he was clothed in a private's blouse, which, if I remember correctly, did not have on shoulder straps. His speech, when not aroused, was slow and drawling ; he did not appear to care for salutes and the men began to regard him as one of them ; he had their confidence and affection, and they willingly followed him. As our regiment was marching this day, he was along side of it, and a newspaper man who had some previous acquaintance with him, remarked : " If you have got as good a division as you had regiment at Bull Run, it will make some dead rebels before long." The general smiled and drawled out, " I guess they'll do."

Monday, the 19th, we marched about five miles and camped, it was said, near New Kent Court House. There is a little church on a hill not far from this camp, and the story was current that Washington was connected with some affair that took place there, I have forgotten what it was. This camp was but a short distance from White House, where, it was said, the Confederate General, Lee, had large possessions.

Wednesday, the 21st, we marched at 6 a. m., and made ten miles and went into camp on the York and Richmond Railroad, about eighteen miles from Richmond. Saturday, the 24th, we marched in the direction of Cold Harbor, a point rather than a place, and about seven miles from Richmond. Indications multiplied that before long the two great armies would lock horns, and prove which was the best man of the two.

On the 26th, Porter, with a part of the fifth corps, had a brush at Hanover Court House. Our people took quite a number of prisoners, and, on their way back, passed by our camp. They gave us to understand there were a sufficiency left back to do up the business for us.

Wednesday, the 28th, the 61st was taken out in the vicinity of Fair Oaks, as a guard to an engineer, who was mapping out the roads. They came in sight of rebel camps, and were treated to a few harmless shells. I was not with the regiment, being in charge of the camp guard.

On the afternoon of May 31st, heavy cannonading was heard on our left, across the Chickahomeny river. For a week, or more, the men had been constantly under arms, so to speak. Three day's rations were kept in the haversacks ; arms and ammunition were frequently inspected ; orders were given warning the men to be in their places and prepared to move at a moment's notice ; so, when the first sound of battle was heard, the men, almost of their own accord, formed on the color line, equipped for a march, where ever it might be to. In a few minutes aides were going from division to brigade, and from brigade to regimental headquarters, and soon the regiments had their orders to march.

For some days before there had been heavy rains which had raised the Chickahomeny river from a low, sluggish stream into a broad, deep, swift running river. As soon as the army got into its then position; by which it was divided by the river, several bridges were built to more effectually reunite the army. The Second Corps had two such bridges, Richardson's being some distance below Sedgwick's. Each division was started for its own bridge. Richardson's was two feet under water ; the leading brigade forded through on this bridge, waist deep in the water. Our brigade was ordered to cross on Sedgwick's bridge. It was floored with small logs laid side by side on log stringers. This bridge seemed to be resting on the water and as we marched over it some of the logs would roll and dip in a manner to shake confidence in its stability, but we crossed on it all right.

I remember seeing a brass gun stuck in the mud on the other side, and the men working to release it. All of this time the sound of battle was ringing in our ears, and its volume indicated that it was one of consequence.

This change of bridges delayed the first division. Sedgwick got up in time to take a hand in the fight of May 31st, but it was after dark and not far from 9 o'clock when our division stacked arms. Some of our men went over the battle field that night and helped care for the wounded. My duties as acting orderly required my constant presence with the company. All was painfully quiet; we did not so much as hear a sound from a wounded man.

The next morning at four o'clock, the men were quietly ordered up. No fires were allowed, so the breakfast was moistened with cold water. After eating, the companies were equalized, and after furnishing a detail to some of the other companies, Company C had forty-one men, indicating that there were four hundred and ten muskets present for duty in the regiment. We were on a part of the battlefield of the day before, and there was considerable of the debris of the battle lying about. The brigade—Howard's—was closed in mass by regiments, the 61st on the left. The waiting for a battle to open is always a trying time for troops. When a movement, or action, is under way the dread leaves. So now, while we were standing with arms in hand watching for the fi.st sign, and straining to catch the first sound we were an anxious multitude.

After a while a section of Pettit's battery was placed at a corner of the field we were in, and by the woods, presently a few shots were fired—possibly as a signal—then came a scattering musketry fire, then a volley on the right of the line, then a rapid increase, and soon the most tremendous infantry fire I ever heard. There was no cannonading, but it was the fearful crash of musketry, where thousands of guns on each side were getting in their work as rapidly and viciously as possible. Orders were now received for the advance of our brigade, and the regiments started out on the double quick. Action of any kind, though it took us towards the enemy, was welcomed. In a short time the railroad was reached, and the 61st was deployed along the track. I cannot assert of my own knowledge, but presume the other regiments of the brigade were in line of battle on this track.

At this point the railroad ran through a piece of woods, and we, though facing occasional bullets from the enemy, could see but a short distance ahead of us. While in this place waiting further orders, Col. Barlow, himself, went forward into the woods to learn more of the situation.

From the stray bullets coming over some of our men were hit. It came to the mind of one, or a few ingenious men in the ranks, that a recumbent posture would conduce to safety, and he, or they, at once took it. This hint was taken up by others, and in a very short time every man was flat on his belly. Presently the Colonel appeared, and, perhaps, looked twice for his regiment he had left standing. He at once roared out, " Who ordered you to lie down? Get up at once." And every man was on his feet. Then the order came, " Forward, guide center. March ! " and we entered the woods.

At this point the timber was quite heavy; there was considerable small growth, and under foot it was swampy. It was impossible to maintain a good line. In such an advance the naturally courageous will press forward, and the naturally timid will hang back, and the officers and file closers have their hands full to urge up the laggards.

In my place as orderly I was directly behind Lieut. Wm. H. McIntyre, commanding my company. Next to me, on the left, was Corporal Willey, an old friend from my town. As we were working our way to the front he spoke to me, and said, " Charley, am I hurt much ?" I looked up and saw the blood running down the side of his face, and that a part of his ear had been shot away. I said, " No, nothing but a part of your ear is gone," and we pressed forward.

Soon we came upon the 52nd N. Y., I think of French's Brigade, lying on the ground in line of battle. I suppose they had exhausted their ammunition and were waiting for our appearance. We passed over them, and advanced a few rods, when the order was given to halt. Then strenuous efforts were made by our officers to get the men up in the ranks and to dress the line; while this was going on no firing was had on either side. I did not see a rebel, and did not think one was within musket shot. Lieut. McIntyre stood in the Captain's place, and I immediately behind him in the place of first sergeant. Suddenly a tremendous volley was fired by the enemy at short range, which was very destructive. McIntyre sank down with a deathly pallor on his countenance. He said, " I'm killed." I stooped down and said, " Lieutenant, do you think you are mortally wounded?" He replied, " Yes, tell them I'm killed." He never spoke again.

A corporal in the next company was shot through the head and fell on to McIntyre's body. I drew up my gun, fired, and then threw myself down behind these two bodies of my friends, loaded my gun, raised up and fired it. This process I repeated until the firing ceased. It was a ghastly barricade, but there was no time for the display of fine feelings. The call was to defeat the enemy with as little loss to ourselves as possible.

I cannot say how long this firing continued, but the time did come when our shots were not replied to, and it was evident we had a clear front. While the firing was in progress I saw a sight that in all of my subsequent experiences was not equalled in shockingness. Sanford Brooks, a stalwart man of my company, and from my town, was shot through the head. The bullet entered at the side and just behind the eyes, and went through in such a manner as to throw the eyes fairly out of their sockets. The wound did not produce instant death, but destroyed his reason. The blow did not fell him to the ground—he stood upright with his gun clinched in one hand, his sightless eyes bulged out of his head, and he staggering about bereft of reason. He lived for a day or two, talking constantly of camp life, and the things that were on his mind before this fatal shot.

After the firing had ceased, orders were given to get together and change position. I did not know that Second Lieutenant Coultis was wounded, and called for him. I was informed that he had been wounded early in the battle and had gone to the rear. This left me in command of the company, and I gathered up the fragments and marched them off.

Illustrating the liability of false information and impressions to stand for facts, is the belief entertained by Gen. O. O. Howard, that Lieut. McIntyre helped him off the field when he was wounded in this battle. Some years ago the General wrote an interesting series of articles for the *National Tribune* concerning his campaigns. In describing the battle of Fair Oaks, he stated where he was when he received the wound that necessitated the amputation of his right arm. In the course of his statement he said that Lieut. McIntyre helped him off the field. This I knew beyond peradventure to be a mistake, and I wrote the *Tribune* an account of the matter so far as McIntyre was concerned, and said my object in so doing was to help put some man in the right who might claim that he had done this service for Gen. Howard.

(In June, 1897, the class of 1894 of Colgate University set up a tablet in the library building in memory and in honor of the sons of the University who had fallen in the war of 1861. Gen. Howard was hired to be present and deliver an address on the occasion. In it he referred to McIntyre and said, after telling how he was aided by McIntyre at Fair Oaks, "He gave his life for me." I was present and heard him make this statement. I took the trouble to write him a full statement of the affair and tried to convince him that he was wholly mistaken in supposing that McIntyre aided him personally that day. In reply I received a short letter to the effect that he so well knew every

officer in the 61st that it could not be possible that he was mis.
taken. I showed this letter to a number of our officers, who
knew nearly as well as I do that Gen. Howard is wrong, in fact.
I need not add, that without exception they agree with my recollection of the matter. Probably no event of consequence will
ever hinge on the truth or error of my statement of this matter.)

Doubtless, as in other human affairs, every person has experiences in battle peculiar to himself and his individual tempera-
ment. In this first real meeting of the enemy, my own,
imperfectly described, were as follows : As soon as the first volley
was fired all dread and sense of personal danger was gone, the
death of the two men, one in front and the other to the right of
me produced no shock of horror. I seemed to regard it as the
to-be-expected thing, and, as I have above said, I loaded and fired
my gun from behind their dead bodies as unconcerned as though
it had been in a sham battle. I now remember, that when the
firing ceased, I was unaware of the strain and excitement I had
been under, until we were ordered to move, when I found that
I was in a tremble all over.

The Confederates had planned wisely, but they failed in
working their combination, and were, I believe, fairly
beaten. Before this battle, Col. Barlow was rated highly for
his *military scholarship*, after the battle he was recognized by his
superior officers as *one of the bravest of the brave.*

In this battle the regiment lost over twenty-five per cent.
of the number present, including the Lieut.-Col., two captains and several lieutenants. (Fox's " Regimental Losses "
makes the number 110).

Later in the day word came to me that a wounded man
wanted to see me. I went back a few rods and there found
my personal friend and townsman, Edgar J. Willey—the
man who had lost a part of his ear before we became engaged.
He had been hit several times, but the one mortal wound was
through his lungs. Every breath he drew was an effort, and
the inhaled air in part went out of the wound with a sicken-
ing sound. As I came up to him he smiled and held out his
hand. I expressed deep sorrow for his condition, but he said
it was all right, he had no regrets. He told me that he could
live but a little while, and requested me to write to his people

and say that he hoped they would not mourn for him. His bible was opened and lying on his breast. He lived for a day or two, and was buried on the field where he fell fighting, like the brave soldier he was.

After the battle the sun came out with southern vengeance. We left our tents and camp equipage at our late camp, and, to make the situation more comfortable, and to guard against sun stroke, the men began to put up bough huts, and before night we were tolerably protected

The army was in a state of expectancy, wondering whether the enemy would make a fresh attack, or whether we would press forward and follow up what had been gained. If we had known better, as we came to, the halting (not to say cowardly) make up of the commanding general, we would have taken it for granted that we were to sit down and intrench and wait the pleasure of the enemy for a change in the situation.

There was no serious attack for several weeks. The lines were formed and fortified ; breast works, with a ditch in front, were built, with here and there a small fort, or redoubt, in which a part of the field artillery was placed.

Picket duty came about twice a week. The lines were near together; and the men were ugly. No chance was missed on either side for firing at a man in sight, and every day more or less were killed or wounded, on the line.

To guard against surprise, the men were aroused and called out by 3:30 a. m., and took their places behind the works, guns in hand, and there stood till sunrise.

As our camp was in the Chickahomany swamp, the water generally was bad, and soon made itself felt in the health of the men. Hot coffee was served to the men as they stood in line, and later, rations of whiskey were issued to dilute the water with.

So long as there is a trace left of this line of breastworks, the exact location of the camp of the 61st can be fixed, as it was just in rear of the line, and half of the regiment was on one side of the railroad track and the other half on the other.

Stonewall Jackson was on his way to aid Lee. On June

26th he appeared, and the Confederate attack opened on our right at Mechanicsville.

Friday evening, the 27th, a part of our division was sent to Porter's aid. He commanded the right wing of the army.

Saturday, the 28th, orders were received for all sick to be sent to the hospital, and for all extra baggage to be turned into the quartermaster. At about 10 a. m. we struck tents and marched down the line to the left, and went to work throwing up rifle pits at right angles with the line of works. This, was, I suppose, in anticipation of the enemy getting possession of the redoubt to the right and raking the line. After a little this was abandoned and we went into the woods in the rear. There we cleared the ground so that a line of battle could be formed. We remained in this position till after dark, when we returned to the old camp ground behind the works. We simply lay on the ground with accoutrements on ready to act in a moment. All night long baggage and artillery trains were rumbling to the rear. The great siege guns that were mounted at this point were loaded on cars and their carriages burned.

By this time there was no doubt in our minds that McClellan's proud advance had come to a halt, in fact, that the pendulum was swinging the other way. About daylight Sunday morning, the 29th, our division began moving up the railroad track away from Richmond and in search for another base. We soon came to the commissary depot of the army. Here were piled million's of dollars' worth of supplies—hundreds of thousands of rations were to be cremated, the torch had been applied to the mass and the work of destruction was well under way. Some of our men slid out of the ranks and went to this stock of stores and helped themselves to whatever they saw that they wanted. They came back with their rubber blankets loaded with sugar; which they divided among their comrades.

After some maneuvering, our brigade was formed in a piece of woods, and we fought what was called the Battle of Peach Orchard. The only loss we sustained here was from the enemy's artillery. Their advance was stayed sufficiently for our retreating troops, and trains to get by ; then our corps fell back to Savage Station, where we again formed line of battle and awaited the approach of the enemy. Before dark a determined attack was made. It was handsomely repulsed.

It has been stated that at this place Gen. Heintzelman, commanding the third corps, told Sumner that the orders were to fall back; thar Sumner protested, and insisted that the Army of the Potomac should retreat no further, but, on the contrary, should attack the Confederates; that Heintzleman finally had to tell the old man that, having delivered the orders, he could act on his own responsibility, as for himself he would fall back as directed ; and that Sumner replied he supposed he would have to follow, but he had not been brought up to retreat from a victorious field.

Those who are ready with reasons for faults and failures in the affairs of mankind, may now lay it to Providence the selection of McClellan as commander of the Army of the Potomac, on the ground that a brave and competent general would have defeated the rebels too soon, and reconstruction would not have been as thorough as it was in the end, owing to the more complete exhaustion of the Confederates. For myself, I have no opinions on such deep subjects. I simply know his selection as a fighting commander was a terrible blunder.

We remained at Savage Station till about 9 p. m., when the retreat movement through White Oak Swamp began. It was very dark. It had rained sufficiently to make the roads very slippery, and, in addition to their being filled with infantry, there was the artillery, and hundreds of baggage wagons to be got over this piece of road before daylight. Owing to the condition of the soil, almost everyone had frequent falls. The column moved at a snail's pace, probably on an average of not over a mile an hour. We were on our feet all night, crossing the corduroy bridge that spanned the stream at the further side of the swamp as daylight began to show in the East. The ground beyond the swamp was a bluff some 20 or 30 feet above it, and on the brow of it our guns were placed later in the day. Back of the bluff was a large, open field, which was literally packed with artillery and baggage wagons. We were marched into position and allowed to lie down. For one, I was so nearly exhausted that I got onto the ground without taking off my knapsack, and at once went off into sleep. About 8 a. m, we were called up and made our breakfast. At this time the baggage wagons were getting out as fast as possible.

About 11 a. m. our pickets reported the advance of the enemy, and in a short time two or three of their batteries opened a lively fire. There were then, perhaps a hundred wagons in this open field. The shelling had a quickening effect in clearing it of all teams permitted to go to the rear.

Our batteries were quickly placed in position and returned the fire. A portion of my brigade, including my regiment, was placed in support of this artillery. While the cannonading was going on, Colonel Barlow was sitting on his old bay horse near to the guns, observing the situation as cooly as if it had been a sham battle. We lost at this place a number of men. This artillery fight lasted I should say for an hour, then tapered off. We still lay behind the guns, and in support of them until near sundown. Then the retreat was resumed. I think the 61st N. Y. was among the last to leave the position.

It was a scorchingly hot day. The sun was never brighter. No air stirred, but the light soil, powdered into fine dust, rose up in clouds that made the march a hardship. For a time we moved slowly, hearing cannon in the distance. Presently, for some reason, the order came to "Step out," which meant quicker time and longer strides ; and a little later the order was to "double quick." Pretty soon we passed squads of cavalry posted along the road, that didn't seem to be doing anything in particular. In those days the cavalry was not what it came to be under Sheridan.

Further on we came to fragments of infantry that showed they had been where war was in practice. Many wounded were about, and disabled artillery was numerous. Before us was a piece of heavy woods; just before entering it on the right, was a long, story-and-a-half building, that was I think, but I am not certain, a tavern. About this building were many wounded—very likely it was in use as a hospital.

The regiment entered the woods on the double quick. The

'road was arched over head by the meeting of the outstretching limbs. As darkness was coming on, it looked like entering a tunnel. Men, singly and in squads, were making their way to the rear, some sound and whole, but many with wounds. As we met these men we were greeted with statements, prophecy and advice. I remember hearing, " This is a tough one." " You'll catch hell, if you go in there!" " You'd better dump those knapsacks, you'll not want them at the front!" I had made up my mind to.that effect, and was putting my hand back to unhook the knapsack strap when Isaac Plumb came up to me and asked what I was going to do. I replied that I was going into the fight without incumbrances. I was impressed with the belief that we were to have a desperate struggle, and, I think, I never felt more like it than I did at this time. I pitched the knapsack to one side, and Plumb did likewise.

I think our regiment had on the field about two hundred men divided for working purposes into four companies. One of these field companies of some fifty men, under Captains Mount and Broady, were not with us. They had been detached and sent off on some special work, so that Barlow had, I judge, one hundred and fifty men. The first company was commanded by Captain Wm. H. Spencer. He was when he enlisted in Broady's company, a student in the freshman class of Madison University. He was appointed orderly sergeant of Company C., and retained that place until his promotion to a lieutenancy in Deming's Company I. On the death of Captain Brooks he was made captain of company G. He was one of the best officers in the regiment. I was at the head of the regiment as we were now advancing along this wooded road. Suddenly the head of a column came in sight and very near to us, and at once the head files of this regiment sent a volley into our regiment. The effect was to make the 61st fall back on itself, so to speak. Col. Barlow was some ways down the line, and there was imminent danger of a stampede on our part for a few seconds. Some of us near enough to the head of the column to take in the situation, enlightened the other regiment and our men, as to the facts, and we passed one another without further damage. I do not know that anyone was hurt by this unfortunate fire, but there were a number of close calls. I remember that one man had his canteen shot away, and others bullets through their clothing.

The further we advanced the clearer came the sound of battle. As we were thus pressing on, I well remember Capt. Spencer saying, as he grimly set his teeth, "Men, we will sell our lives as dearly as possible!" I believe every man of us regarded it as a desperate adventure.

Further on we came to a cleared field of considerable size, in which there were, I believe, one or two small, old buildings, perhaps negro houses. Just before reaching the open field we turned off to the right and came in on the right hand side of the field, and lay down behind the rail fence. While in this situation, a general officer came up and had a talk with Barlow. From what I heard at the time and have since read, I am of the opinion it was Gen. Kearney. I heard him say, "Colonel. you will place your men across that road, and hold it at all cost." Barlow replied, "General, you know I have but few men." "Yes," he said, "but they are good ones." The general, whoever he was, then went off. Barlow at once ordered the men up, and to advance. The fence was passed, then a right wheel made, an advance of some rods, and we were near to the edge of the field and directly across the road. The order was given to lie down. Shortly after this was executed, a voice came out of the woods in front of us, and very near by. It was too dark to see anything, but our ears took in every word of the question asked, "What regiment is that?" At once an Irishman replied, "Sixty-first New York." Then came the command, "Lay down your arms, or I'll blow every one of you to hell." That sentence was scarcely out of his mouth, when Barlow roared, "Up and at them, men."

The command was instantly obeyed. We got in the first volley, and it was doubtless effective. Some of our wounded left on the ground and captured next day, reported, when we next saw them, that there was a large number of dead rebels close up to the line of our field.

As soon as our volley had been delivered the men of their

own accord dropped back a rod or two, lined up and went steadily at work. As I have suggested, it was too dark to see anything within the woods, and, if the enemy could see anything of us, it was just a line.

Our fire was at once returned. As soon as our empty muskets could be loaded the men would take a quick aim at a flash in the woods and let drive. The enemy did the same. In no battle that I was in, did the bullets sing about my head as they did here. No doubt this came from the aim drawn on the flash of my musket. This steady, rapid firing continued till it ceased from the woods, and we concluded that we were victors.

Barlow then directed that the sound men take to the rear those alive, but wounded so that they could not help themselves. A sergeant by the name of Marshall, as I now remember, was badly wounded through the thigh. Another man and I attempted to carry him back. I found that my gun was an obstruction and I laid it down, thinking I could come back and find it, or some other. We carried our comrade to the rear, where quite a number were placed, among them Capt. E. M. Deming, who was suffering from a broken leg. We were close friends, having been together in the winter of '60 and '61 in the Academic Department of Madison University. I stopped to have a little talk with him, believing that there was to be no more fighting that night.

Presently my attention was called to the fact that there was a fresh lining up of men where we had just fought. It was not so dark but that the outline of a body of men could be distinguished in the open. At once the firing from both sides was resumed as brisk as ever. Later on I learned that a part of the 81st Pa. had come to our aid.

I was not long in sensing that my position was not military. Some of my regiment must be in that line, and I was some rods to the rear, and without a gun. I did not propose to go hunting for a lost gun in that darkness and under fire. In looking about, I discovered a gun standing against a tree. I took it, saw that it was loaded, and then conceived the notion that I might make a flank attack on the rebels by myself. The line of battle on each side was but a few rods in length. Where I stood the trees were not thick, and I was a little to the right of the firing. I made an advance movement that brought me nearly up to the line of our men, but, as I said, to their right. I decided that Providence had favored me in providing a good-sized stump just beyond and in the line I proposed to fire. I brought my gun to an "aim," waited for a flash from a Confederate gun, and pulled the trigger. About as soon as could be, after the flash of my fire, came quite a volley of bullets singing around my head, from the enemy's line. I moved closer to my stump for more complete protection, when to my dismay, I found it to be only a body of tall grass. I did no more firing from that position, but fell back in good order.

The fighting soon ceased and our men retired and took position in the road in the woods, but near to the open field. We lay down on our arms. After a while the enemy came up where their wounded were, and we could hear them call out the regiments to which they belonged as they were picked up. Finally matters quieted down and most of us went to sleep.

At the time we called this the battle of Charles City Cross Roads. I think the accepted name at present is Glendale. This position had been during the day desperately attacked by the Confederates and heroically defended by the Federals. If the enemy had succeeded in their purpose they would have cut off a large section of our army and captured property of great value. In my account of the fight written at the time to my people I said, " Barlow got us together in line and found that a good deal more than half of the men were gone, and pretty much all of the officers. Captains Deming, Spencer and Moore lost legs, and Angell was wounded. Lieut. Crawford and Adjutant Gregory were wounded. Col. Barlow and Lieuts. Keech and Morrison were the only officers with us, and some of these had very close calls, all of them had bullet holes in their clothing. Barlow's horse was killed and Keech's scabbard was battered up with one or more bullets. But forty men were together unharmed at the end of the contest."

That my account of this fight may not stand alone as a

stubborn and desperate one, I will quote from the account of it as found in Appleton's Annual of 1862. While it may be obnoxious to the charge of gushiness, to those who were in this fight, by daylight, or in the night, I think scarcely anything can appear exaggerated. It is as follows:

"The advance of the Confederate force was actively resumed early in the morning. Generals D. H. Hill, Whiting and Ewell, under the command of General Jackson, crossed the Chickahominy by the grapevine bridge, and followed the Federal retreat by the Williamsburg and Savage Station road. Generals Longstreet, A. P. Hill, Huger and Magruder took the Charles City road with the intention of cutting off the retreat of the Federal forces. At the White Oak Swamp the left wing under General Jackson came up with the Federal force under Generals Franklin and Sumner, about 11 a. m. They had crossed the stream and burned the bridge behind them. An artillery fire was opened on both sides, which continued with great severity and destruction until night. The result of this battle was to prevent the further advance of the enemy in this direction, which was the single line of road over which trains had passed.

" Late, on the same day, a battle was fought between the forces of Gen. Heintzelman and the main force of the enemy, which attempted to advance by the Charles City road to cut off the retreat. This force was led by Generals Longstreet, A. P. Hill and Huger. The former, however, being called away, the command devolved on Gen. Hill. As the masses advanced upon the Federal batteries of heavy guns, they were received with such a destructive fire of artillery and musketry as threw them into disorder. Gen. Lee sent all his disposable troops to the rescue, but the Federal fire was so terrible as to disconsert the coolest veterans. Whole ranks of the Confederate troops were hurled to the ground. Says an actor in the conflict: 'The thunder of cannon, the cracking of musketry from thousands of combatants, mingled with the screams of the wounded and dying, were terrific to the ear and to the imagination.'

"The conflict thus continued within a narrow space for hours, and not a foot of ground was won by the Confederates.

"Night was close at hand. The Federal lines were strengthened and the confidence of the Confederates began to falter. The losses of his exhausted and wornout troops in attempting to storm the batteries were terrible. Orders were given to Gen. Jackson to cover the retreat in case the army should have to fall back, and directions were sent to Richmond to get all the public property ready for removal. The Federal forces, perceiving the confusion, began step by step to press forward. The posture of affairs at this time is thus related by a Confederate officer: 'The enemy, noticing our confusion, now advanced, with the cry, 'Onward to Richmond!' Many old soldiers who had served in distant Missouri and on the plains of Arkansas, wept in the bitterness of their souls like children. Of what avail had it been to us that our best blood had flowed for six long days? Of what avail all our unceasing and exhaustless endurance? Everything, everything seemed lost, and a general depression came over all our hearts. Batteries dashed past in headlong flight; amunition, hospital and supply wagons rushed along, and swept the troops away with them from the battlefield. In vain was the most frantic exertion, entreaty and self sacrifice of the staff officers! The troops had lost their foot-hold, and all was over with the Southern Confederacy!

"In this moment of desperation Gen. A. P Hill came up with a few regiments he had managed to rally, but the enemy was continually pressing nearer and nearer! Louder and louder their shouts and the watchword, "On to Richmond!" could be heard. Cavalry officers sprang from their saddles and rushed into the ranks of the infantry regiments now deprived of their proper officers. Gen. Hill seized the standard of the 4th North Carolina regiment, which he had formerly commanded and shouted to the soldiers, "If you will not follow me, I will perish alone!" Upon this a number of officers dashed forward to cover their beloved general with their bodies; the soldiers hastily rallied, and the cry, 'Lead on, Hill; head your old North Carolina boys!' rose over the field.

"And now Hill charged forward with this mass he had thus worked up to the wildest enthusiasm. The enemy halted when they saw these columns, in flight a moment before, now advancing to the attack, and Hill burst upon his late pursuers like a famished lion.

"A fearful hand to hand conflict now ensued, for there was no time to load and fire. The ferocity with which this conflict was waged was incredible. It was useless to beg the exasperated men for quarter; there was no moderation, no pity, no compassion in that bloody work of bayonet and knife. The son sank dying at his father's feet; the father forgot that he had a child--a dying child; the brother did not see that a brother was expiring a few paces from him; the friend heard not the last groan of a friend; all natural ties were dissolved; only one feeling, of thirst, panted in every bosom—REVENGE.

"Here it was that the son of Maj. Peyton, but fifteen years of age, called to his father for help. A ball had shattered both his legs. 'When we have beaten the enemy then I will help you,' answered Peyton, 'I have other sons to lead to glory. Forward!' But the column had advanced only a few paces further when the Major himself fell to the earth a corpse. Prodigies of valor were here performed on both sides. History will ask in vain for braver soldiers than those who here fought and fell. But of the demoniac fury of both parties one at a distance can form no idea.

"Even the wounded, despairing of succor, collecting their last energies of life, plunged their knives into the bosoms of foemen who lay near them still breathing.

"The success of Gen. Hill enabled other generals to once more lead their disorganized troops back to the fight, and the contest was renewed along the whole line, and kept up until deep into the night; for everything depended upon our keeping the enemy at bay, counting too, upon their exhaustion at last, until fresh troops could arrive to reinforce us. At length, about half past ten in the evening, the divisions of Magruder, Wise and Holmes, came up and deployed to the front of our army."

As I have suggested, the foregoing quotation is a somewhat florid account of desperate, prolonged fighting.

The following account of the 61st's fight at Glendale is

taken from the *Portland Daily Press.* It is the narration of a leading actor in the battle, and was given at the annual meeting of the Maine Commandery of the Loyal Legion held at Riverton, May 3d, 1899.

"This paper will deal chiefly with my personal experiences as subaltern and Captain in the Sixty-first N. Y. Volunteers during the first and last days of June, 1862, in the Peninsular Campaign, Virginia.

"Omitting the narrative of the regiment's participation in the battles of Fair Oaks, Peach Orchard, Savage Station and White Oak Swamp, we come to the battle in which the writer received the wound which crippled him for life.

"As we drew near to the battlefield of Glendale, we came to a place which tried the courage of us all. I shall never forget that scene. The road ran through an open field which was dotted here and there with dead and wounded men. There were all the grim tokens of the rear of a desperate battle, straggling men, cannon without horses and with broken carriages, battle smoke in the air, and the sound of a gun which was out of sight in front accompanied by the howl of grape shot. We halted here a few moments to give the stragglers time to come up, and to give all a chance to breathe after our exhausting march. Besides the men that were lying around us wounded, others were coming out of the woods in front limping and bleeding. They greeted us with such cheering assurances as "You'll get enough in there," "Better throw away them knapsacks, you won't want 'em in there."

"Before us there was a dark forest of great hemlocks, and I can see yet the lurid light of the setting sun through the trees and the powder smoke ; and I remember that the question came into my mind, "I wonder if I shall ever see another setting sun." I did not, of course, give any outward sign of such thoughts. I had enough to do to inspire my men with courage, telling them we must sell our lives at a high price. But I have heard some of the regiment, who went through many subsequent battles, say that that was the dismalest battle they ever saw.

"Down into the narrow road, through the dark hemlocks

we passed. It was full of powder smoke, which with the dark foilage, shut out most of the daylight that remained. There was a solitary gun away off on our right, whose occasional boom sounded like a knell.

"We came out of the woods on the right side of a clear field where a portion of the afternoon battle had raged, and lay down by the side of the road, conscious that we were in a ticklish place. There was occasional firing over us into the field, and once in a while a bullet dropped near us. But this soon ceased and the battlefield, as a whole, was quiet, and I began to hope that the battle was over. But our colonel was of another mind. He had reported for orders to Gen. Robinson of Kearney's division. The twilight was deepening and the stars were out, when the order came, " Get up men, STEADY NOW, FORWARD, March!" Every man sprang to his feet. Quickly we were over the fence with bayonets at a charge, and when we were well in the field the regiment made a half right wheel towards a piece of woods on the other side. I was neither depressed nor elated, but it was a relief to be in motion with my company. I was simply in the line of duty, responsible for myself and my company. I remember how finely the regiment marched across that field through the shadows and the smoke to unknown horrors beyond. We advanced to within two or three rods of the woods and lay down. It was too dark by this time for us to see whether the woods were occupied or not, but after a brief interval we learned all about it. While we were all on the qui vive, wondering what would come next, a voice broke forth from the woods clear and distinct, " What regiment is that?" Every heart stood still. Who would answer? And what would he say? To my astonishment and dismay one of our men piped out, "Sixty-first New York." Then came the blustering reply, " Lay down your arms, or I'll blow you all to hell." Instantly we were on our feet, and by the time the orator in the woods had finished speaking his little piece our men had poured in a volley before they were ready for us. This must have seriously damaged them, for their return volley was lighter than I expected. There was nothing for us to do however, but to fall back a few rods, loading and firing. We soon halted however, and settled down to the grim game of give and take in the growing darkness. The flashes of their muskets were all that our men had to guide their aim. It was dismal business. Our line grew thinner, and I noticed that my company was melting away before me. Anxious to hurt somebody I drew my revolver and emptied one barrel into the woods, but then considered that I might want the rest for closer work before we got through, and put it up again. Soon I felt a smarting pain in my left knee and sat down a few paces apart to see what made it. Finding it only a buckshot I hastened back to my company, but it took that buckshot wound six weeks to heal. It seems to me now as if I had not been back with my company more than a minute when crash came a blow on my right leg, just above the knee, like the blow of a huge club. There was no mistaking that. I dropped because I had to, and I lay flat on my back so as to avoid other bullets, and waited for further developments. Those were solemn moments for me, and yet not so terrible as one might suppose. They were not at all dreadful. I was just waiting to see if I was going to die from loss of blood, not knowing but an artery was severed. I distinctly remember thinking that I would hardly turn my hand over for the choice, whether to rise presently to a new heavenly home, or to struggle back through unknown sufferings to my old earthly home. But after a few moments the instinctive desire to live in the body prevailed. I saw that I was not going to bleed to death, so I called a couple of men to carry me back to the road away from the firing line. In doing this, one of them put his arms under my knees, and the pain in the wound soon became so frightful that I begged them to lay me down and let me die. They carried me to the road however, a short distance, and there left me.

"So there I lay on my back, looking up to the quiet stars and listening to the combat which was still going on. This is a narrative of personal experiences and feelings, designed for family use, and so it is in order for me to tell how I felt as I lay there. It might be expected that I should say that I was longing to be back in the fight impatient to be leading my brave men up to the muzzles of the enemy's muskets. But if I were to say so I would lie. As I lay there, I was not all smitten by a fit of the heroics nor anything of that kind. I was tired, almost exhausted by the exertion and excitement of the day, two days in fact. And it felt fine to just lie still there and rest. As long as I kept still my wound did not pain me much. I hated bullets and had no appetiate for glory or promotion, and it was a relief to lie there out of range of the detestable mines. Moreover, I had full confidence that my men would give a good account of themselves, whether I was with them or not. There was satisfaction too, in feeling that I was through, that I had kept in the line of duty until I was shot and disabled, and that I had given to my country all that she asked of me in the shooting line of endeavor, and could now take up life again on a new basis. To be sure there were some chances against my getting safe home again, but I had a cheerful confidence that I should be able to pull through somehow. I have often been amused while thinking of my feelings as I lay there across the middle of the road. The prevailing sensation was one of relief. I was no cow-boy or rough-rider. I was just an ordinary patriot and student, ready to bleed and die if need be for my country, but never spoiling for a fight. And I know that many of my bravest comrades were made of the same stuff.

My greatest want just then was water, and that I couldn't get it until a rebel supplied me next morning. Even when our regiment came back to the road where I lay, or what was left of it, no one could get a drop for me. Colonel Barlow came to me after the fighting was over, and showed all the tenderness of a brother, letting me see a side of his nature that I had never known anything about before. He deplored the fact that there was no way by which he could have me carried off and kept within our lines. And so, after having me moved to the side of the road, and after my friends had come and talked with me and bade me good-bye, that splendid little regiment marched away about two o'clock in the morning, and left me to reach home, nearly dead, after about twenty-four days, by the way of Libby prison.

"The Sixty-first New York left about one-third of their

number dead or wouded on that field, including six out of its nine officers, of whom three lost one leg each, and one of them died in Libby prison. Only a month of fighting and its numbers were reduced from 432 to about 150.

" Dropping now the personal narrative, let us in the briefest sketch, follow that plucky little regiment under its peerless commanders.

" See them the very next day at Malvern Hill, again enduring the pounding of artillery until nearly night, and again in open field engaging the enemy under cover of the woods until they had fired 90 rounds per man and were all ready to charge with bayonets if required.

" See them at Antietam, with the ranks replenished from the hospital and recruiting offices, under the cool and skilful leading of their colonel, getting advantage of a wholè rebel brigade where there was a deep cut in the road, and, after slaughtering many of them, actually capturing about three hundred prisoners, more than they themselves numbered. There they lost their intrepid colonel, Barlow, by a desperate wound and subsequent promotion.

" But he was succeeded by a soldier equally brave and gallant, Lieut. Colonel Nelson A. Miles, who in the battle of Fredericksburg led them to the useless slaughter at the foot of Marye's Heights, until a bloody wound in his neck spared the regiment a desperate attempt to get a little nearer than other regiments to the invincible lines of the enemy.

" See them at Chancellorsville, with Miles again leading in a brilliant fight on the skirmish line.

" See the devoted little company in the Wheat Field at Gettysburg, hardly a company all told now—only 93—baring their breasts to the storm of Confederate bullets and leaving 62 of their number, two-thirds, among the killed and wounded.

" Nearly a year later, after 600 recruits had made it nearly a new regiment, see it keeping up its old reputation for hard fighting in the Wilderness campaign, losing 36 at Corbin's Bridge and 13 at Po River, and then at the famous Bloody Angle at Spottsylvania, having a place of honor and peril in one of the two leading brigades which scaled the rebel works and took between three and four thousand prisoners. Then see them at Cold Harbor sacrificing 22 of their number in a bloody repulse in that useless slaughter.

" In the siege of Petersburg see them in repeated engagements. At Ream's Station, when one regiment after another of recruits gave way, Walker tells us that Gen. Miles, commanding a division, ' calling up a portion of his own old regiment the Sixty-first New York which still remained firm, threw it across the breastworks, at right angles, and commenced to fight his way back, leading the regiment in person. Only a few score of men--perhaps 200 in all—stood by him; but with these he made ground, step by step, until he had retaken Dauchey's battery, and had recaptured a considerable portion of the line, actually driving the enemy into the railroad cut.''

" At last at Farmsville, only a day before the end of the struggle, this regiment sealed its devotion to the flag by the loss of four killed, including one captain, and twelve wounded.

" In the round up of Lee's army culminating at Appomatax, two divisions of the corps were commanded by Sixty-first men. Barlow commanded one and Miles the other, and between them they fought the last infantry battle of the Army of the Potomac.''

" In Colonel Fox's admirable analysis of the Regimental Losses during the Civil war, he shows that the Sixty-first New York came very near having a place among the forty-five regiments that lost over two hundred men, killed or mortally wounded in action during the war. Its actual loss was 193, including 16 officers. He says: ' The Sixty-first had the good fortune and honor to be commanded by men who proved to be among the ablest soldiers of the war. They made brilliant records as colonels of this regiment, and, being promoted, achieved a national reputation as division generals. The Sixty-first saw an unusual amount of active service and hard fighting. It served through the war in a division that was commanded successively by Generals Richardson, (killed at Antietam), Hancock, Caldwell, Barlow and Miles, and any regiment that followed the fortunes of these men was sure to find plenty of bloody work cut out for it."

In the place we were marched to we lay down. Very soon the fifty men under Captains Broady and Mount, who had been detached, joined the forty or so of us making all told a fighting force of from ninety to one hundred men. Most, if not all the men, except those on guard, went to sleep.

About two o'clock a. m. of July 1st, we were quietly awakened and cautioned to make no noise. The order to move was whispered and we started silently.

A good part of our way was over a road through the woods. No artillery or wagon trains were in the way, and we shoved along at a good pace. Most of the canteens were empty before the last battle, and now the men were suffering for water nearly as much as it was possible for them to. I do not know of any of our troops following us, and it is my belief that we were the last of the Army of the Potomac to go over this road, as we were, the following December to cross the pontoon bridge at Fredericksburg.

I suppose we made a march of from three to five miles, when we came into open country, not far from three o'clock a. m. The light was just beginning to show in the East. We did not know the locality or the name of the place if it had one. We saw that a part of our army at least was massed here. Later on we came to know that it was Malvern Hill, where a great battle was soon to be fought. I am glad we did not know it before it came. In our ignorance, we assumed that now the fighting was over for a time, and we would be given a chance to recuperate after the strain of the past week. As soon as arms were stacked details for water gathered the dry canteens and went in search of the much needed fluid. Those who could, stretched out on Mother Earth for another nap.

As soon as the sun was up the men stirred themselves, made coffee and ate such food as they had in their haversacks —hard bread, and boiled salt pork, or beef. At such times the soldier's menu is not elaborate, and he is satisfied if there is enough of it to prevent the pangs of hunger.

We were occupying an open field with other troops of our corps, without protection from the broiling sun. The intense heat was not as bad as a battle, but some of our men were used up by it. I think it must have been in the neighborhood of 10 a. m. when some of our men spoke out: 'There's the reb's planting a battery.' Every eye was turned in the direction indicated. It was plain to be seen that artillery was being placed, but, at the distance, I could not distinguish the uniforms, and I declared that they were our men. My wisdom did not have long to maintain itself, for in a short time shells were dropping in on us in a way no friend would shoot.

Now preparations were rapidly going on for a great battle —the last of an historic series. Ammunition was being distributed to the infantry, boxes of cartridges were brought to us and opened while we were standing this shelling. Capt. Broady superintended the distribution. Every man filled his cartouch, and then Broady made us take from forty to sixty rounds in the haversacks. He declared as he went up and down the lines, when some of the men grumbled at the quantity, 'Men, you may be glad to have them before you get more.' After a while our batteries silenced the guns that had been making it disagreeable for us.

While we were in this place a matter transpired that has left an unfading impression on my mind. A member of our regiment, who had been much of the time detailed, and had acted as hostler for some of the field officers, but was now with his company, came up to Colonel Barlow with a woe-begone countenance and told him that he was sick and not able to be in the ranks, and said that the doctor thought he ought to be permitted to go to the rear. No doubt Barlow had noted the use this man had been put to, and, where he believed a soldier was managing to escape danger and find a soft place, he always endeavored to make it as unpleasant for that man as possible. The Colonel was not in an amiable frame of mind. He was on foot, old "Billy" had been killed the night before, and he felt like having a dialogue with someone. He asked this man some questions which satisfied him he was a coward. His wrath broke out vehemently. He cursed and swore at him and called him a variety of unpleasant and detestable things and then he began to punch him with his fist wherever he could hit. Finally he partly turned him around, and gave him a hearty kick in the stern and said: " Damn you, get away from here! You're not fit to be with my brave men." The fellow departed as fast as his short legs would carry him. I knew of no other man presenting an excuse or asking for leave of absence that day. I believe every man of us preferred to meet the rebels rather than the vocal scorn and denunciation of Barlow. I believe he did not know what personal, bodily fear was, and he had no consideration for a coward.

I met Barlow in New York in LaFayette Post Room, at the time Sixty-first Regimental asociation was formed. I made this remark to him: "I never went into a battle without an effort of my will, and always expected to be wounded or killed." He said in his quiet way, " I never felt so, I never had an impression that I was to be hurt." In the address at Hamilton, N. Y., in 1897, before referred to, Gen. Howard said that Gen. Barlow was one the bravest and coolest men he ever saw in battle.

After a while our brigade was moved forward and about half way up a rise of ground—it was hardly a hill—at the top of which were an old house and barn. We were ordered to lie down in support of a battery in front that was doing a lively business. I remember that before getting down I spread my rubber blanket to lie on. The fragments of the exploded shells came showering down upon and about us, presently a chunk large enough to have laid me out a harmless corpse came tearing through my blanket, but in a spot not covered by my body. Every now and then along the supporting line a man was knocked out. It was at this time that Ralph Haskell, a Hamilton boy, and another lying beside him had their brains knocked out by these shell fragments. They were but a few feet from me and I saw the whole bloody business.

About this time a remarkable freak was perpetrated on the body of Capt. Broady. He was standing, when in an instant he was thrown to the ground with great force, and he lay there quivering as if life were the same as extinct. Col. Barlow saw him fall and ordered his body taken to the rear

This was done by a number of men, who remained by the body to observe the passing of the last breath, when to their surprise the captain opened his eyes and, with his slightly Sweedish brogue, inquired if he was much hurt. The men replied, '' Why yes, you're all knocked to pieces.'' The captain wiggled about some and then asked, '' How do you know men, do you see the blood run?'' They had to answer '' No.'' By this time his consciousness had fully returned. He directed the men to help him onto his feet and soon came back with his old-fashioned nippy gait. Barlow had regarded him as ticketed for the '' happy hunting ground'' and when he saw him walking back to the line, he was quite surprised. He looked him over for a moment, and then said to his regiment, '' Men, give Capt. Broady three cheers, he's a brave man.'' This we did with a will. When we got to a place where an examination could be had, it was found that Broady had been so struck by a piece of shell that it went through his overcoat, and then rotated in such a manner as to cut the tails off from his dress coat, so that, after we got to Harrison's Landing the captain went about dressed in that frock coat with the skirts cut off. In other words he was supporting a jacket.

Shortly after this episode we were ordered forward up the slope to the level ground and where the before mentioned old house and barn were. We again lay down. The enemy were shelling these buildings at a terrific rate, the rattle and crash of the shells into that woodwork made the hair fairly stand on end. As we first lay down, it was found best to have the men face about. This was done without getting up and countermarching, but by facing around and bringing the rear into the front rank. The officers crawled back as best they could, and the sergents did the same. I was making my way to the rear when one of the officers turned up his head and said to me, '' Where in the devil are you trying to get to?'' The tone indicated that he thought I was trying to sneak off. This made me mad, and I snarled out, '' I'm trying to get into my place. If you think I'm afraid, I'll go to the front as far as you dare to!'' Within the following year this officer came to know me well, and had, I believe, confidence that I would not seek to avoid a place of danger.

After a time this artillery attack on our position ceased, and we were ordered forward to the brow of the hill on the other side. Here we had planted the greatest continuous row of cannon I ever saw set for work in a battle. I would not be surprised to have it said by authority that fifty of them crowned the brow of this elevation. Our position was immediately on the right flank of this line of guns.

The Seventh New York, a German regiment, was formed on the left of the Sixty-first N. Y., and in the rear of the artillery as a support. This German regiment joined our brigade after the battle of Fair Oaks. It came to us from Fortress Monroe, about one thousand strong under Col. Van-Shack. He had, I believe, served in the German army and was a fine appearing officer, but a full blooded German organization was not, in this country in those days, on a par with "Yankee" troops. A sprinkling of Dutchmen was all right. We had in the Sixty-first Germans and Dutchmen, who were the peers as soldiers, of any in the regiment, but this Seventh regiment when it went into action jabbered and talked Dutch to exceed in volubility any female sewing society ever assembled. As they came up and got into position the volume of jabber almost overcame the rattle of musketry and the roar of artillery. I am certain their conduct did not favorably impress our men. If the German Emperor's army is not made of grimmer stuff than I saw exhibited in pure German regiments in our army, I would not fear the result in matching them with Americans from the North or the South.

It was said, and I suppose it was so, that in front of us was Magruder and the story was current that he had served his men with gun-powder and whiskey. Many stories are on the wind at such times that are no nearer the truth than lies. I do not believe the rank and file very often had their courage braced up with whiskey.

The battle of Malvern Hill was a splendid fight for our side, and I firmly believe if we had been commanded by a brave and confident man like Grant, Sherman, Sheridan, Thomas or by some of the corps commanders of the Potomac

Army, Gen. Lee might have been pushed at least into the defences of Richmond. But McClellan was on the James protecting the gun boats, and composing a scolding letter to the president—probably.

From our position on the brow of the hill, it was open ground for a distance and gently sloped off to the woods. Time after time the enemy formed for the purpose of making a charge on us, but no sooner did they appear than this immense line of artillery opened fire, which no troops in the world could withstand. In aid of the artillery fire, the infantry posted so as to have a chance, poured in volley after volley. Col. Barlow practiced here that which I never saw before or after in battle—volley firing by ranks. Then he changed it to firing by files and then to firing at will which is as often as you please. This tremendous storm of missiles held the confederates at bay. They did in a feeble way reply to our fire, and we lost in killed and a large number wounded. At times our firing was so rapid that the gun barrels became heated to the point that they could not be grasped and the men held their guns by the sling strap. I had some personal experiences in this battle that were unique in my service. Our muskets were the Enfield rifle, an English gun, much like the Springfield. They were, of course, muzzle loaders, breech loaders then were the exception. The Minnie bullet had no device for cleaning out the barrel, and after a dozen shots it would become foul, and often it was difficult to ram the bullet home. After I had fired my gun a number of times, in attempting to load, the bullet lodged half way down. I made desperate efforts to send it home but to no purpose. I found a stone large enough to pound on the end of the ramrod, but the only effect seemed to be to set it the snugger. It was the wrong place to hesitate in. I capped the tube, drew up the gun and pulled the trigger expecting an explosion. The kick was strong but I did not discover any damage to the gun—doubtless the barrel was injured. I picked up another gun left by some dead or wounded man and resumed my work. After exhausting the cartridges in my cartridge box, I had my hand in my haversack for a fresh package, when I felt myself severely hurt in the arm. The sensation was, it seemed to me, as if a red hot rod had been run over it. I supposed I was badly damaged and brought up my arm so as to examine it in the growing darkness. I found that a bullet had taken the skin off from my wrist, a piece as large as a cent, and only to the depth to allow the blood to slowly ooze through. The momentary hurt of this slight flesh, or skin wound was more severe than I experienced a year later when the bones of my leg and arm were shot through. The next day on the march to Harrison's Landing, where we halted long enough for lunch, I discovered that this bullet had gone through my haversack, cutting off a piece of the rim of my tin plate, and, in its passage had journed through my bags of coffee and sugar and had compounded them considerably.

In this fight George Joyce of Co. C was seriously wounded through the arm, so that he was obliged to go to the hospital. He was a singular person—small in stature, illiterate, and until he became known for what he was, regarded by all as a braggadocio. I do not remember that his remarkable qualities were observed until the night before at Glendale. It was during the second attack, while I was off on my flank movement, that Barlow ordered the men further forward. A man spoke out, "We will follow the colors." Joyce had them, or took them as a volunteer—as he was but a private— went to the front with them, jabbed the staff into the ground and said, "There's your colors! Come up to them!" and the men obeyed. For this act Barlow complimented Joyce, and then and there promoted him to an orderly sergeancy in in another company. I shall mention Joyce again, when he next appeared with the regiment at Fredericksburg.

The fighting was prolonged until late into the evening, and the usual amount of ammunition taken into the battle was exhausted before we left the field. I remember Barlow's saying, "If the enemy make another attack, we will meet them with the cold steel."

Gradually things quieted, and about 12 o'clock we fell back a few rods and lay down on our arms. We were not disturbed till daylight, when we could see that the retreat movement was still in progress.

Finally we took our turn in the march. We had not gone far when one of the men came to me and said that our flag was back where we had rested after the fight, and he asked if he had better go back for it. I said to him, " By all means get the flag!" He did as requested, and that same bunting waved on a good many hard fought fields afterward. I do not know, but presume that this flag was finally replaced by another. It was, even then, much delapidated, and at Antietam it was mercilessly pierced and torn. The road we finally reached, for Harrison's Landing soon entered a narrow place between two bluffs. Two or three columns were using the road and when they came to this sort of gorge it became almost a jam. I remember hearing a few guns fired at this time, and the effect on the men was to cause them to crowd faster to the rear. At the time it came to my mind with painful force, " If the rebels should attack us with a brave, fresh division, they would stampede us." From what I have since read, I think each army considered itself whipped and was glad to get into a place of safety!

At all events, we were not further molested in our march to Harrison's Landing. We reached the place about noon and went into camp. The James River, from ten miles below Richmond down to Bermuda Hundred, is about as tortuous as a river ever runs. At that point it widens out, a distance of from one to two miles ; much of that space is, of course, shallow water.

The next day the enemy run down a battery or two, on the south side of the river, and gave us a lively shelling. Our division general, Richardson, wanted to change the location of some of us, and became very impatient at the slow movements of the men. He roared out: " *Make haste, men! make haste! every minute is an hour!* and the men hustled at a livelier gait.

Richardson steadily grew in the esteem of his men. The story had got noised about that while we lay in camp just before Fair Oaks, a loafer about his headquarters addressed insulting language to a woman who was employed in doing certain domestic work and who followed up the army. The general heard the vile talk of the fellow from his tent. He hastily made his appearance, and, in words expressed his disapproval of such conduct, and, in acts he kicked the offender a number of times with such power as to raise him at every kick a number of feet into the air, and then sent him to his regiment. That offence was not again committed at those headquarters.

In a few days the army was in position at Harrison's Landing. The James at this point bends in slightly on the North bank and is very wide. A line of breastworks was thrown up surrounding the encampment. I presume the place was made secure against any attack from the enemy. As McClellan was an engineer officer, he was, doubtless, good for entrenchments, if for nothing else.

On the Fourth of July President Lincoln came to us and we were reviewed by him and the commander of the army. Mr. Lincoln was dressed in black clothes and wore a silk hat. That hat on the top of his six feet four made him a very tall man. Recently the newspapers have published a story purporting to have been told by Gen. Lew Wallace, to this effect: He was one day at the White House. It was just after the Army of the Potomac had got to its new base. The president was so obviously sad and cast down that the general ventured to remark upon it. The president took him across the room where no one could hear what he said and there told him that in an hour he was to start for the Army of the Potomac to prevent its commander from surrendering it to Lee. While I think McClellan was a fearful incompetent, I am slow to believe, if the above ever took place, that Mr. Lincoln had good grounds for his belief. In those early years of the war, no doubt, much was reported that, later, would not be listened to Whatever may have been the moving cause, the president was with us that day, and we cheered his presence to the echo.

During the weeks we were here encamped, we went to the James for occasional bathing, but we did not have facilities for washing our clothes in boiling water. The result was that we were all well stocked with body lice. The men generally were diligent in picking off and destroying the lives of these little animals by pressure between the thumb nails. The slaughter of all in view one day, left enough back in concealment so that the next day's hunt was always rewarded by abundant captures.

The only time I was excused from duty while in the service on account of sickness was while we were in camp here. One day I took a company of sick to the doctor. I staid by till he had passed out the last dose. We had three remedies, one of which would hit any possible case. They were opium pills, castor oil and quinine. The pills cured all bowel troubles; castor oil lubricated and opened up the internal functions, and quinine cured everything else. I remarked to the doctor that I would rather like to experience the sensation of being excused from duty and placed on the sick list for one day. Nothing in particular was doing, so the obliging surgeon said, "All right, you may go to your quarters sick and be excused from duty for one day." I am now glad to say, that was the first and last time I was ever so favored.

In this camp I was subjected to discipline by Col. Barlow. The evening before, on dress parade, I was named to take charge of a police detail from the Sixty-first, which was to report at brigade headquarters the next morning at five o'clock. I had slept but little during the night. Toward morning I fell into a drowse, and was awakened out of it by the reveille. I hurried out of my tent and was getting my detail together, hoping that the colonel would not notice my tardiness. I got to the place of rendezvous the first of any one in the brigade, and had to wait for an hour before a start was made. Our party worked through the forenoon, picking up all litter, looking after sinks, burying dead animals and doing whatever came in view to make our section of the country sanitary and look tidy. This performed we returned to our respective regiments. Having dismissed my detail, I was going to my tent when Sergeant Major Greig sang out, "Sergeant Fuller, the colonel says you may consider yourself under arrest, and you will confine yourself to your tent." I knew of course the reason for this. I stayed within for a couple of days, and then wrote a statement of the case and got a drummer to take it to the colonel. It came right back with an endorsement that if I had any communication to make, it could be done through the regular channel. I then sent the paper to Lieut. Keech and he forwarded it to the colonel. In a few moments I received from him a line that I was relieved from arrest and could resume my duties. These disciplinary matters were needful to keep the men up to their duties, and the organization instructed, and in working order.

One evening Barlow took the regiment and started for the front. We passed our intrenchments, and, it was said, we marched in the direction of Malvern Hill. We advanced a number of miles, discovered no enemy and returned to camp before morning.

About the eighth of August signs appeared that a change was coming. The seige guns were withdrawn and shipped, as were the heavier camp equipage and extra baggage. Aug. 16th about noon we broke camp and moved out, we did not know where to, nor where for. It proved to be a march down the peninsula. The first day out we made but about four miles, and halted near a corn field. The corn was fit for roasting and the men had a feast. I suppose the strict rules of McClellan's army, probably, were violated as there was some foraging done.

August 17th we made twelve miles, and passed Charles City Court House. Inexcusable vandalism was here committed. The books and records of the county seat were scattered about in profusion. Many documents two hundred years old were passed about, and there were those with Washington's signature. We crossed the Chickahomony, I was told, near its junction with the James, on a pontoon bridge, I should think one-eighth of a mile in length. It was the longest stretch of bridge of the kind I ever saw.

The road we took on this march was not the one by which we went up, on our way to the Richmond we did not see until about three years after. The country does not vary much from prairie level. The soil is light, with no stone in it to speak of. In a dry time, with considerable travel it powders up so that in going through it the dust rises in almost solid columns. A good part of the Potomac army, horse, artillery, foot and baggage trains, had preceded us. This made the dust as deep as it could be. Much of the road was through forests. I well remember this march from the dust experience. It exceeded anything I ever heard of. We would march for long distances when a man could not see his file leader—the dust so filled the air as to prevent seeing. Of course, the men had to breath this air. The nostrils would become plugged with the dust so moistend as to make slugs. Every now and then the men would fire them out of their noses almost as forcibly as a boy snaps a marble from his fingers. I remember having serious forbodings that taking in such quantities of road dirt would cause lasting injury. I do not know that my apprehensions of evil from this cause were ever realized. I suppose the dust that got into the lungs worked out in some way.

Aug. 19th we passed through Williamsburg, the site of William's and Mary's College and the capital of the colony in the days when Patrick Henry told the House of Delegates that, "Caesar had his Brutus, Charles the First his Cromwell, and George the third—might profit by their example." At this time the place was very delapidated. As I remember there was but one good looking house. The place had been well fortified against our approach as we were going up in May.

Aug. 26th we reached Yorktown and went into camp on the same piece of ground we had used about three months before. Those three months had wrought great changes in our circumstances as a regiment and an army. "We had met the enemy' and he was NOT ours. After stacking arms I wandered around and in so doing came across a quantity of split peas, which doubtless had been left by our army on the upward march. With others I concluded to try a change of diet and prepare a banquet for mastication that evening. I took enough of the peas to cook my quart cup full, and patiently sat by the camp fire through the evening looking after the cooking. It was quite late when they were boiled tender. I was hungry from the waiting, they touch-ed the spot in the way of relishing, and, in a brief time the bottom of that old quart cup was bare. The prevailing complaint with the men was diarrhoea, and I was one of the prevalents, so to speak. This was not hygenic food for such a case, and, without further words, I was not very well the remainder of the night. The weather had been hot for that latitude. The next morning it was like the furnace of Nebuchadnezzar—several times hotter than it had been. I felt more like being petted by a nurse than to shoulder my traps and tramp. I could hardly stand, but to go was a necessity. We made that day a march of twenty miles, I think. Not being able to step out squarely, but rather drag and shuffle along, I began to chafe badly, which made the marching very painful. I kept up with the boys till towards the close of day and about a mile from where camp was made, when I grew dizzy. I saw all sorts of colors. I staggered out one side and went down like a bundle of old clothes. I lay there in semi-consciousness, until the rear guard came along, when I was accosted with the question, " What are you here for?" I said I couldn't go another step. " Well, but you must. Come, get up, or we'll prick you." I made the effort under this pressure, and did work my way over that mile to where the regiment had stacked arms. This was the first and only time I ever failed to be present with the regiment when it stacked arms and I was with it.

On this occasion whiskey had been issued. The first time since it had been given us when stationed behind the breast-works at Fair Oaks. Some one of my friends had saved for me my ration and it was a big one. I should think there was nearly a tumbler full of it, and it was the rankest, rottenest whiskey I ever saw, smelled or tasted. My legs were raw and bloody from the chafing, and I was sick all over. I divided my whiskey into two equal parts, one half I used on the raw flesh, and it took hold like live coals. This done I nerved myself to drink the balance, and, by an effort, kept it down. I rolled up in my blanket, went to sleep, and so remained till roll call next morning. When I stirred I was somewhat sore and stiff, but was essentially well, and made that day's march as easily as I ever did. During this day's march we had one of the hardest showers I was ever out in. In a short time every rag on the men was drenched. Shortly after the sun came out and before halting the heat of the sun and bodies had dried everyone, and we felt as though we had been washed and ironed—thoroughly laundered. This day's march brought us to Newport News, where shipping was at anchor to transport us somewhere.

We took a steamer which headed for the Potomac. During the time since we left Harrison's Landing Lee had cut across the country and was making it warm for Gen. Pope in the Shenandoah. The army of the Potomac, in place of following in the rear of Lee, made its slow way down the peninsula, and then shipped up the Chesapeak and Potomac, unloading at Aquia Creek, Alexandria, etc.

On the 27th of August, at about two p. m., our steamer stopped at Aquia Creek landing. We went ashore and marched inland some five or six miles and went into camp. Here we heard artillery firing. No doubt from some one of the numerous conflicts Pope was then having.

About ten p. m. orders were given to "fall in." We returned to the Landing, took our steamer, and proceeded up the river to Alexandria. Here we again went ashore, and were marched out to the grounds of Camp California, the same spot we had wintered on. We remained in this camp till about 6. p. m. of the 29th of August, when we marched and went into camp near Arlington. Here we remained till about three p. m. next day, when hurried orders were received to march with nothing but guns and ammunition. Our shelter tents were left standing, and our blankets in them, but the men had hungered and thirsted too much within the last six months to leave haversacks and canteens. It may be that this order to take nothing but our arms and cartridges had got distorted in transmission from headquarters, as it would seem that no general officer would start men out without food and water. At all events, the men knew enough to disobey such an order.

Heavy firing was going on in the direction of Centreville, some twenty miles away. We had not drawn shoes since setting out on the peninsula campaign, and the soles of our shoes were worn lamost through. This road to Centreville was full of small round stones and they were hard on our feet. We stepped out on a rapid march and made very few halts till we were within sight of the heights of Centerville. Then the column was halted, and the weary men lay down in the road where they were halted, and went to sleep.

Early in the morning we were aroused and met an endless

stream of men hurrying to the rear. These were of Pope's army who the day before had fought the battle of Second Bull Run. It has always been a mystery to me why old Sumner and his second corps were not in the fight. Surely from the time we landed at Aquia Creek on the 27th, there was abundant time to have gone to Pope. In place of doing that we were lounging around for about three precious days. Gen. Porter may have been wrongfully convicted of disobedience to Pope's orders. Gen. Grant came to be of that opinion, but I have never seen anything to make me doubt that the, so to speak, McClellan officers were so disgruntled at the practical retirement of their "beloved chief" that they gave no cordial support to Gen. Pope. I never supposed that Edwin V. Sumner was one of them, and I have always believed that he was ever ready To Fight for the Union, whoever commanded.

We pushed out beyond the old fortified line held by the enemy the winter before, and there the Second corps was deployed in line of battle. This morning there was a steady rain that drenched us. When night came there were no blankets, and it was cold and the ground soaked. The men lay down together as closely as they could pack themselves, but it was an uncomfortable night. Under such hardships men become impatient and reckless, and prefer a fight to the discomfort. We occupied this ground next day. Towards night a very hard rain came down, which gave us another rinsing. We moved back a piece where there were large fresh brush piles. These we fired and, while they lasted we had comfortable warmth. Then we lay down on the wet ground and courted sleep. About 9 p. m. orders were passed along to get up and move. We were all night in making a very few miles.

The next morning we learned that we were near Chantilla, where the night before we had a brush with the enemy in which we sustained a serious loss in the death of Gen. Philip Kearney. He was one of the men that had won the reputation of loving the terrors of battle. He had lost an arm in Mexico, but single handed he would go into a fight, as an eater would go to a banquet. Kearney was a grandson of

Judge Watts, who owned land and had a house in the town of Sherburne, and, in his boyhood days, Kearney spent some time here with his grandfather.

We lay in the vicinity of Fairfax Court House through the day. Towards evening we marched to Hall's Hill, not far from Chain Bridge. On the way we got a few shells from the enemy, which hastened our footsteps.

Sept. 3rd, we crossed Chain Bridge and marched about five miles to Tanleytown, where we remained until Sept. 5th. At this place our tents, knapsacks and blankets came to us, and were received with thanks. Campaigning in August and September in Virginia without shelter and blankets was a hardship. Such exposure uses up men as speedily as fighting. While in this camp the men lived " sumptously every day." It was but five miles from Washington, and the pie and cake vendors were out in sufficient numbers to supply all demands.

On the 5th we were marched about nine miles and camped near Rockville, a flourishing village in Maryland. Our company was placed on picket. The next morning I discovered a cow near by, and persuaded her to allow me to barrow my old quart cup full of her milk. As I drank it I vowed, if ever I got home, I would make a specialty of drinking fresh milk as long as I relished it.

Sept. 6th we marched beyond Rockville about six miles and formed in line of battle. Batteries were posted and, so far as we knew, there was to be a fight, but it blew over. Such " scares" are of frequent occurance in a soldier's experience. We remained in this place until the 9th, then marched about six miles and camped. After all was quiet some of my friends went out, and late returned with a supply of potatoes and " garden sass. " On the 10th a march of four miles was made. On the 11th five miles, and we camped at a small place called Clarksvill. Here our company was detailed as provost guard. We remained at this place through the day. Someone purchased or TOOK a duck. We had a most delicious meal in the shape of a stew. Potatoes, onions and such like, were boiled with it, until the whole substance was a tender mush. I know that after that meal the feasters were almost too full for utterance.

At this time the little Sixty-first regiment was commanded by Colonel Barlow and Lieut. Col. Miles. For field purposes the regiment was divided into three companies. First, the company commanded by Capt. Angel and Lieut. Keech, in which was my company C. (Capt. Broady was at this time away on sick leave.) Second company was commanded by Capt. Walter H. Maze and the third by Capt. Geo. D. H. Watts. There were about 35 men to the company. In other words, there were but one hundred and five muskets for all of these officers to direct. I have often remarked on what I deemed to be a very idiotic policy pursued by the authorities of the State of New York at this time, and I have believed that Gov. Morgan was equally to blame with Seymour. What I refer to is this. When troops were to be furnished by the State of New York, these governors would, as I understand it, organize new regiments of raw men, when there were scores of veteran organizations in the field with the rank and file greatly depleted. The Sixty-first was not the only skeleton New York regiment in the field. This regiment always had enough officers to have commanded in battle five hundred men, and, by experience in battle, they had come to know how to handle them. It would have been an immense saving to have filled up and made these weak regiments strong by sending to them from rendezvous camps recruits by the fifties. The new men would have rapidly taken up and learned their duties in the field from contact with the men who had learned what they knew from actual service. Then, the officers in these old regiments had got weeded out. The cowards and weaklings had, generally, been discharged, and their places filled by SOLDIERS who had come from the ranks. I was never informed why this common sense plan was not adopted. I imagine that the powers were not so much for the good of the cause, as to make themselves strong politically throughout the state from the appointment of a great number of officers. In state politics it was as powerful as in national politics to have the appointment of a horde of civil and military officers. If a governor was influenced by such considerations and understood how detrimental to the country such a course was, morally he was a traitor, and ought to suffer the odium of treason committed. Some of the states had the wisdom and the patriotism to adopt the plan of keeping the regiments at the front filled up. It was a crying shame to allow Frances C. Barlow to command a regiment carrying but a little over one hundred muskets. Someone should have seen to it that the Sixty-first should never have been long with less than five hundred men in the ranks.

On the tenth we marched ten miles, passing through Hyattstown. On Saturday, the 13th, we marched through one of the finest towns I had seen in the South--Frederick, Md. We camped on the further side of the town. Sunday we hoped would be a day of rest. In the morning a field of ripe potatoes was discovered close by, and notwithstanding McClellan's savage order against taking anything, in a short time that field had upon it, almost a man to a hill of potatoes. It did not take long to dig that field. Our anticipations of a day of rest, with a vegetable diet, were disappointed. The bugles sounded "Strike tents," and we were soon on our way on the road over South Mountain.

At this time fortune favored "Little Mac." Gen. Lee's plan of campaign fell into his hands, and he was fully informed as to the purposes of the Confederates. Some generals would have made good use of this important knowledge, but it did the Union commander but little good. This general order of Lee directed one of his corps to take Harper's Ferry. I think the common sense of most people would have said, "Now you concentrate your army and fight and destroy Lee's two-thirds, before he can concentrate." If that would have been good strategy, McClellan did not use it.

We had an uphill march out of Frederick. Having gained the crest of the first range of hills, we halted, and our regiment was deployed on a picket line. While lying about waiting for something to turn up, we discovered a farm house to the front, and sent several of the men to see what could be purchased for the table. In a short time they returned with milk and soft bread. Porter E. Whitney of my company was one of them, and he expressed his contempt for their simplicity in not charging more than they did for the amount furnished.

While we were preparing to cook our foraged potatoes and eat the provision from the farm house, we noticed the movement of troops in line of battle moving up the mountain side ahead of us. Batteries went into position and opened fire, then our men would make a rush, and take and hold an advance position. Then the artillery would follow, and shell the enemy from the advanced position. We had a fair view of this battle of South Mountain, which was regarded as a brilliant affair. It was fought I believe, under the immediate direction of General Reno, who was here killed. While we were thus safely viewing this battle, and watching the potatoes boil, Lieut. Keech made a remark that amused me, and has remained fresh in my memory. We were just ready to squat around the camp fire and lay to, when he said, "Well boys, we'll have one more belly full anyway." Just about as he finished that sentence, the order came "fall in and march." I took my cup of boiled potatoes and carried them in it until we halted at the foot of the mountain about 9 o'clock in the evening, when I ate them in the dark, rolled up in my blanket and went sweetly to sleep.

Monday, the 14th, we were up in good season, and started up the mountain. We advanced in line of battle and frequently halted for the skirmishers to advance, but we met with no opposition, and soon were on the top of the ridge. We passed several field hospital stations, where operations had been performed, and where had been left numerous legs and arms that had been amutated. These sights are not refreshing to advancing troops—they make them think too much of what is likely to happen to any one of them. As we were about to go down the other side of the mountain, a battery of our flying artillery went by on a canter, and we followed after them on the "double quick." Having got down to level ground we soon passed through Boonsborough. Our brigade was in advance this day, and we were close on the rear of the enemy and saw the last of him go over the hill ahead of us. At the time we did not know that we were on the banks of the—to be—celebrated Antietam. We followed the Boonsborough road nearly to the river. At this point the shore on our side was lined by a ridge twenty to thirty feet in height. We turned to the right and deployed part way down the rise of ground back from the river. At first our light artillery took position in front of us on the crest of the hill. By the next day these light guns were replaced by twenty pounders. Most of the time we were in this place artillery firing was going on between these guns and those of the enemy bearing on them. But little damage was done to us as the shells of the enemy went over us. About midnight of this Monday we were aroused and directed to march with our arms, and to leave everything else but our canteens, and to be careful to make no noise.

Lieut. Col. Nelson A. Miles commanded the expedition. We went through the fields to the left of the Boonsborough road, then aimed for the river. When we came to the bank which was high and steep, we worked our way down to the level of the road, entered it and crossed the bridge, which was a single arched stone bridge. We then carefully advanced some distance along the road, met nothing, turned back and made our way into camp. At the time the boys were confident the enemy had again gone on.

Tuesday, the 16th, we remained in the same place. There was much firing by the heavy battery in front of us, which was well replied to. A rebel shell went through the body of Col. Miles's horse. After dark we were moved to the right and near by the ford, which we crossed the next morning.

The morning of the 17th opened somewhat hazy. By 8 o'clock the artillery firing was heavy and Hooker was making his attack on the right. From where we stood we saw the effect of the artillery. Buildings were set on fire by our shells, and the air was full from their broken fragments. While we were in this place a rumor started down the line that we had been detailed as body guard to McClellan. This comforting statement did not last long, as, in a little while we were ordered to move. We forded the river, which in places was a foot deep. On the other side we halted, took off our shoes and stockings, wrung the loose water out of them, and put them on again. I cannot, of course, give the direction of our march. Col. Barlow had under his command, besides his own regiment, the Sixty-fourth New York, which had about two hundred men—giving him a force of about three hundred and fifty.

I remember in making our advance through the fields we came to a depression through which the bullets were flying briskly. It was not a wide piece and we passed it with lively steps. Now in front of us the ground rose gradually into quite a hill, and rather to our right the Irish brigade was deployed and was engaged. We moved up a ways and formed in line of battle. Where I came a solitary tree was near by. Quite a way to the front and to our left was a good sized tree heavily leaved. Out of that tree soon came rifle shots and our men were beginning to show wounds. Capt. Angell, who was a very good officer had told his friends that he knew he would be killed in this fight. I was within a few feet of him when he dropped with a bullet through his head. Barlow called out for half a dozen good marksmen to clean out that tree. Among the number to respond to this call was W. H. Brookins of company G. The boys fired rapidly into the tree and in a brief time two Confederate gentlemen dropped to the ground, whether dead or alive I do not know, but we had no more trouble from that source.

In the meantime the fight of the Irish brigade had come to be very hot. They were in our plain sight and we could see them drop and their line thin out. The flags would go down but be caught up, and down again they would go. This we saw repeated in each regiment a number of times. While this was going on, Gen. Meagher called out to Barlow, "Colonel! For God's sake come and help me!" Barlow replied that he was awaiting orders, and would come to him as soon as he could. The musketry fire in front of us had now mostly ceased, in consequence of the destruction of the Irish brigade. Finally, orders to advance came to us, and we went forward with a rush, Barlow in the lead, with his sword in the air. We crossed a fence, and came up a little to the left of the ground just occupied by the Irishmen. Our appearance renewed the fire of the enemy.

As we got a view of the situation it was seen that the rebels were in a sunken road, having sides about four feet in height; this formed for them a natural barricade. Barlow, with the eye

of a military genius (which he was) at once solved the problem.
Instead of halting his men where Meagher had, he rushed
forward half the distance to the rebel line, halted and at
once opened fire.   We were so near to the enemy, that,
when they showed their heads to fire, they were liable to be
knocked over.   It did not take them long to discover this,
and for the most part, they hugged the hither bank of this
sunken road.   Barlow discovered that by moving his men to
the left and a little forward he could rake the position of the
Confederates.   This he did, and our firing was resumed with
vigor.   The result was terrible to the enemy.   They could do
us little harm, and we were shooting them like sheep in a pen.
If a bullet missed the mark at the first it was liable to strike
the further bank, and angle back, and take them secondari-
ly, so to speak.   In a few minutes white rags were hoisted
along the rebel line.   The officers ordered " cease firing," but
the men were slow of hearing, and it was necessary for the
officers to get in front of the men and throw up their guns.

Finally the firing ceased, then Barlow ordered the men
forward.   They advanced on a run, and when they came to
the bank of the sunken road, they jumped the rebels to the
rear.   Those able to move were glad to get out of this pit of
destruction.   Over three hundred were taken, who were able
to march to the rear.

The dead and wounded were a horrible sight to behold.
This sunken road, named by some writers "The Bloody
Lane," was a good many rods long, and, for most of the
way, there were enough dead and badly wounded to touch
one another as they lay side by side.   As we found them in
some cases, they were two and three deep.   Perhaps a
wounded man at the bottom, and a corpse or two piled over
him.   We at once took hold and straightened out matters
the best we could, and made our foes as comfortable as the
means at hand afforded--that is, we laid them so that they were
only one deep, and we gave them drink from our canteens.
After some time spent in this way, a body of the enemy was
discovered deployed to our right. Barlow at once formed the
command nearly at right angles to the position we had just
held, and advanced us.   We passed a fence, and soon open-

ed fire on this new force. In the meantime the enemy had placed a part of a battery in position that began to rake our line with canister. Charges of this deadly stuff went in front and in the rear of our line. Some of those discharges, if they had happened to go a little further to the front or the rear, would have destroyed our two little regiments. Such close calls often happen in battle. We held our ground, and after a while the rebels fled from the field. One of them was considerably in the rear of his comrades and as he was exerting himself to get out of harms way, our men concentrated a fire on him. He was on plowed ground, and we could see the dirt fly up in front, and rear, and on each side of him as he was legging it. He was escaping wonderfully, and I felt as though he was entitled to succeed. I called out to our men and entreated them not to fire at him agian, but without avail. The shooting went on, and, just before he was out of range, down he went, killed perhaps, possibly wounded.

About this time Col. Barlow was dangerously wounded from a canister shot, and Miles took charge of our affairs. The firing had again quieted. He directed me to take two men and go forward, part way through the corn field in front, and watch and report any appearance of the enemy. If I am not mistaken, I took Porter E. Whitney and George Jacobs of my company. We went forward half way through the corn field, which was for the most part trampled down. We arranged the broken stalks so as to be partially concealed. After a time to our front and right, and on the brow of a considerable rise of ground, a body of officers appeared on horseback, and with glasses took observations. We discussed the propriety of aiming at these Confederates and giving them a volley. I finally concluded it was best not to take this responsibility, as it might bring on an attack that we were not ready for. In a short time these men disappeared. I sent back one of the men to report what we had seen. Very soon he came back with the word to join the regiment. Longstreet in his book entitled "From Bull Run to Appomatox," speaks of looking the field over about this time and from near this location, so, I judge, it was he and his staff that we had such a plain view of.

Our command under Miles, was, about 5 p. m., drawn back and established just in rear of where we made our first fight. Our Division General, Richardson, was this day mortally wounded. He had the entire confidence of his men, as a brave and skillful soldier, and his taking off was deeply lamented. Barlow was supposed to be mortally wounded, but he recovered, and in a few months came back a brigadier, and was given a brigade in Howard's Eleventh Corps.

Gen. Hancock was assigned to our division. By this time he had won the reputation of being a hard fighter, and this he justly held through the remainder of the war.

In this battle I had a hand in an amusing incident that is worth recording. There was in company A, a little Irishman about 40 years of age by the name of Barney Rogers. This man had been recruited by our New York party the spring before. He did not write, and, knowing me from the first, had come to me to do his correspondence. When we started to take the place of the Irish brigade, I noticed that Barney appeared to be holding up his pants, but I made no inquiry as to the reason for his so doing. When we took our first position in advance of where the Irishmen had fought, and began firing, Barney had to use both hands, and his predicament was at once revealed. He had held up his pants by a strap around his waist without suspenders. This strap had given out, and that accounted for his holding up performance. When he began loading and firing he had to " let go" and leave the pants to follow the law of gravitation. Soon his ankles were swathed with these low down breeches, and he was effectually teddered. I was here and there, doing my duty as a sergeant. I had not noticed Barney's predicament till he called to me in a tone of urgency and said, " Charley, cut the damned things off!" I took in the situation in an instant, and in less time than I can write it, jerked out my large knife, opened it, grabbed the waistband, made a pass or two, and one leg was free. I said, " You can kick the other leg out." He made a few passes, and from the top of his stockings up his legs were bare. A good breeze was blowing sufficient to take. away the smoke from our guns, and sufficient to flap his unconfined shirt tail. I remember calling Ike Plumb's attention to it and our having a good laugh over it. Barney continued his fighting, and was with the men in the grand charge that captured the rebels in the sunken road. He was also in his place in the second attack we made. While the firing was at the hottest I heard a man cry out, and I looked just in time to see Barney throw his gun, and start off on his hands and one leg—the other leg held up. The last I ever saw of him he was pawing off in that fashion. I suspected that in some way he had got a shot in the foot. Years after this occurance, I wrote a series of articles for THE SHERBURNE NEWS, and in one of them gave this account. As soon as the paper waa out, my comrade, Porter E. Whitney came into my office. He was in this battle and, I supposed, he knew about this affair. He had read the account, and I said to him, "Of course, you remember it?" To my chagrin, he replied, "That is the first I ever heard of it!" I said to him, "That will leave me in a fine situation, people will ask you if you remember the Barney Rogers incident, and you will say, "No," and the enquirers will conclude that I have been telling a "Jim Tanner yarn." "Well," he replied, "I can't remember what I never before heard of."

Some days after this, Whitney came to me and asked if I knew Barney Rogers's address. I said, "No." He told me it was in the roster lately published by the regimental association. I found it and at once wrote to the address, and briefly inquired if he was the little Barney Rogers that I cut the breeches off from at Anteitam. In a few days I got a letter from Barney written by his son, in which was the statement, "I am he." It went on to say that he was hit under the big toe by a bullet that had probably gone into the ground, struck a stone and glanced up, taking him as indicated. He said that he went off the field in the way I have described, until he was out of danger, and then hopped along as best he could. Finally, a soldier from a Connecticut regiment met him, who had an extra pair of pants, which he gave to Barney. He got inside of them as speedily as possible, and then waited for an ambulance, when he was taken to a hospital, and finally discharged.

In this battle our flag was shot through a good many times

and the staff had a bullet go through its center just above the hands of Sergt. Hugh Montgomery, who was carrying it.

All through the 18th we remained in position, hugging the ground. The picket lines of the two armies were near together, and were blazing away at one another on every opportuity. Our line of battle was so near to the picket line that anyone showing himself would be fired on. One of my company, Julius C. Kelsey of Smyrna, was killed while on this duty. The Sixty-first lost in killed and wounded about one-third of its number, and so was again reduced to the size of a full company.

Some one discovered on the 19th for "Little Mac," the "Young Napolean" that the enemy had, during the night, fallen back and crossed the Potomac at Shepardstown. If the commander of the Army of the Potomac had been a brave and competent general, he would have disposed of Lee at this time. As I have before stated, McClellan knew while we were at Frederick that Lee was to divide his army, sending a third of it to take Harpers Ferry. He ought to have known when we overtook Lee at Sharpsburg that he had but part of his army there, and he ought, with his entire force, to have made a rushing attack at once. In place of that, he dawdled for two days, giving Lee all the time he wanted to take Harpers Ferry from the old, incompetent Miles, and to unite his army to fight him. There was good brave fighting at Antietam, but it was by piece meal—a division or corps here and a division or corps somewhere else. The best work done that day by Caldwell's brigade, was by the Fifth New Hampshire under its able colonel, Edward Cross, and by the Sixty-first and Sixty-fourth New York under Col. Barlow. In support of this statement all authorities agree. McClellan in his report says, "The brigade of Gen. Caldwell, with determined gallantry, pushed the enemy back opposite the left and center of this (French's) division, but, sheltered in the sunken road, they still held our forces on the right of Caldwell in check. Col. Barlow commanding the Sixty-first and Sixty-fourth New York regiments, advanced the regiments on the left, taking the line in the sunken road in flank, and compelled them to surrender, capturing over three hundred prisoners and three stands of colors.₊ ₊ ₊Another column of the enemy, advancing under shelter of a stone wall and corn-field, pressed down on the right of the division; but Col. Bar-low again advanced the Sixty-first and Sixty-fourth New York against these troops, and, with the attack of Kimball's brigade on the right, drove them from this position. Our troops on the left of this part of the line having driven the enemy far back, they, with reinforced numbers, made a de-termined attack directly in front. To meet this Col. Bar-low brought his two regiments to their position in line, and drove the enemy through the cornfield into the orchard be-yond, under a heavy fire of musketry and a fire of canis-ter from two field pieces in the orchard and a battery farther to the right, throwing shell and case shot." Vol. 19, Series 1, Off. Records, pages 60-61.

Palfrey, in "The Antietam and Fredericksburg," at page 100, says, "Col. Barlow particularly distinguished himself in these operations of Richardson's division. He had under his charge the two right regiments of Caldwell's brigade, the Sixty-first and Sixty-fourth New York. As Caldwell's line was forcing its way forward, he saw a chance and improved it. Changing front forward, he captured some three hun-dred prisoners in the sunken road to his right, with two colors. He gained this advantage by obtaining an enflad-ing fire on the Confederates in the road, and it seems to have been owing entirely to his own quickness of percep-tion and promptness of action, and not to the orders of any superior officer. He was also favorably mentioned for his action in helping to repel another attempt of the lines to flank Caldwell on his right, and also for contributing large-ly to the success of the advance, which finally gave the Fed-erals possession of Piper's House."

Walker in history of the Second Corps at page 114 says " As the line presses onward toward Piper's, Barlow, com-manding the consolidated Sixty-first and Sixty-fourth New York, sees, and at once siezes a tactical opportunity. Chang-ing front forward at the right moment and on the right spot he takes in flank a body of the enemy in the sunken road, pours a deadly volley down their line and puts them to flight, capturing three hundred prisoners with two flags. A determined struggle follows: the enemy even assume the aggressive against Caldwell's center, but are beaten off by the quick and resolute action of Barlow, who falls desperately wounded."

Longstreet in his Bull Run to Appamatox, at page 266, says, " The best tactical moves at Antietam were made by Generals McLaws, A. P. Hill, Gibbon, and Patrick (Confederate) and Colonels Barlow and Cross (Union)." At page 252 he refers to Barlow as the " aggressive spirit of Richardson's right column."

Gen. Caldwell in his report, says, " The brigade advanced steadily over the crest of the hill behind which the enemy were posted, receiving and returning a heavy fire. We broke the line of the enemy along our entire front, except on the extreme right. Here there was a deep road, forming a natural rifle pit, in which the enemy had posted himself, and from which he fired on our advancing line. After the enemy opposed to my left and center had broken and fled through the cornfield, Col. Barlow by a skillfull change of front, partially enveloped the enemy on his right, and, after a destructive inflading fire, compelled them to surrender. About 300 men and eight commissioned officers, among them an aid to Gen. Stuart, were here taken prisoners by Col. Barlow * * * * * On the right, Col. Barlow, finding no enemy in his immediate front, saw a considerable force moving around his right. Moving by the right-oblique to a hill about three hundred yards distant, he opened a severe fire upon them, when they broke and fled. Thus both attempts to turn our flanks had been foiled by the skill and quickness of Colonels Barlow and Cross, and the determined bravery of the men * * * * I cannot forbear to mention in terms of highest praise the part taken by Col. Barlow of the Sixty-first New York volunteers. Whatever praise is due to the most distinguished bravery, the utmost coolness and quickness of perception, the greatest promptitude and skill in handling troops under fire, is justly due to him. It is but simple justice to say that he proved himself fully equal to every emergency, and I have no doubt that he would discharge the duties of a much higher command with honor to himself and benefit to the country."

Barlow's own report is as follows:

General Hospital, Keedysville, Md., Sept. 22, 1862.

Captain: I have the honor to make the following report of the Sixty-first and Sixty-fourth New York volunteers in the battle of Sept. 17th inst. Both these regiments were under my command on that day, and had been for some time previous. On going into ac-into action our bridage was formed on the left of the Irish brigade. We remained about fifteen minutes under the fire of the enemy's sharpshooters which my sharpshooters returned with effect. I lost then Capt. Angell and one or two men killed. By order of the staff officer of Gen. Richardson, we then moved to the right, in front, and formed behind the crest of the hill, and bravely engaged the enemy and fired destructively. With the assistance of the fire of the regiments on our right and left, we broke the enemy on our front, who fled in disorder through a cornfield, suffering severely from the fire of our and the Irish brigade, my regiments being on the right of the brigade. The portion of the enemy's line which was not broken, then remained lying in a deep road, well protected from a fire in their front. Our position giving us peculiar advantages for attacking in flank this part of the enemy's line, my regiments advanced and obtained an enflading fire upon the enemy in the aforesaid road. Seeing the uselessness of further resistance, the enemy in accordance with our demands threw down their arms, came in in large numbers and surrendered. Upwards of three hundred prisoners thus taken by my regiments were sent to the rear with a guard of my regiment, under charge of Lieut. Alvard of Gen. Caldwell's staff. On this occasion my own regiment, the Sixty-first New York, took two of the enemy's battle flags, which have been forwarded to Corps headquarters. A third flag was captured by the Sixty-fourth New York, which was lost by the subsequent shooting of the captor when away from his regiment.

" After these events, my regiments, with the rest of our line, advanced into the cornfield, through which the enemy had fled, beyond the deep road above referred to. No enemy appeared in this field. Our troops were joined together without much order— several regiments in front of others, and none in my neighborhood having very favorable opportunities to use their fire. Seeing quite a body of the enemy moving briskly to the right of our line, at no great distance, to attack us on the flank, my regiment changed front and moved to the crest of a hill on our right flank, occupying the only position where I found we could use our fire to advantage. This was to the right of the Fifty-second New York of Col. Brook's brigade. We engaged several regiments of the enemy with effect, some being posted on the edge of a cornfield behind a stone wall surmounted by a fence; others were posted still farther to the right, on the edge of the cornfield. The enemy at length retreated quite precipitately under the fire of the troops on our side, together with another body of Federal troops, which attacked the enemy in turn on their flank and rear. I am unable to state who these last named troops were. On retiring from this position, the enemy renewed their attack on our old front. My regiments again changed front, and advanced into the cornfield, which we had left, to assist in repelling the flank attack of the enemy just mentioned. Beyond this cornfield was an orchard, in which the enemy had artillery (two pieces to the best of my knowledge.) From these pieces, and from others still farther to our right, they had been pouring a destructive fire of shell, grape and spherical case shot during the above mentioned engagement of our infantry.

" After thus forming our line on the right of the Fifty-seventh New York of Col. Brooke's brigade, I was wounded in the groin by a ball from a spherical case shot, and know nothing of what subsequently occurred. My own regiment, the Sixty-first New York, behaved with the same fortitude and heroism, and showed the same perfect discipline and obedience to orders under trying circumstances for which I have before commended them, and which causes me to think of them with the deepest affection and admiration. The Sixty-fourth behaved steadily and bravely. Of the officers in my own regiment, I commend to special notice for bravery, coolness, and every soldierly quality in action, Capt. Walter H. Maze, Co. A; First Lieut. Willard Keech, Co. G; Second Lieut. Theo. N. Greig, Co. C; Second Lieut. F. W. Grannis, Co. B; Lieut. Col. Nelson A. Miles has been distinguished for his admirable conduct in many battles. The voice of everyone who saw him in this action will commend better than I can his courage, his quickness, his skill in seeing favorable positions and the power of his determined spirit in leading on and inspiring the men. I have the honor to be, Captain, your very obedient servant,

FRANCIS C. BARLOW,

Col. 61st. N. Y. Vols. and Comdg, 64th N. Y. Vols.

Capt. George H. Caldwell,

Capt. and Asst. Adj. Gen., Caldwell's Brigade.

The report of General Miles is as follows:

Headquarters Sixty-first Regt. New York Vols.

Camp near Sharpsburg, Sept. 19, 1862.

" I have the honor to transmit the following report: On the 17th inst., about 9 o'clock the Sixty-first and Sixty-fourth N. Y. Vol., under command of Col. Barlow, were ordered to form on the left of the Irish brigade while they were engaging the enemy. We remained there about twenty minutes, during which time we lost one captain and several men. We were then ordered to move by the right flank in rear of the Irish brigade until we came to their right. Here we came to the front, and moved up and over the hill under a heavy fire of musketry and a cross fire of artillery. We found the enemy lying in a road or ditch just under the brow of the hill. The regiment, however, steadily moved up and over the hill in the most determined manner and spirit, breaking the center of the enemy's line and killing or wounding nearly all that left the ditch to make their escape through the cornfield. Then we improved the advantage we had gained by changing front forward on first company, thereby flanking the rest of their line. The Colonel gave the command, " Cease firing," when I called out to them to surrender. They at once threw down their arms and came in. I think by this movement we captured two hundred and seventy-five or three hundred prisoners. I detailed one company to guard them and turned them over to Lieut. Alvord, with two stand of colors.

The enemy were then out of sight in the front, but were discovered moving around our right. The Colonel then gave the order " Right shoulder, shift arms," and moved to the right oblique to another hill about 300 yards distant, and commenced firing to the right upon the enemy. He fired about twenty rounds here, when the enemy's line broke in perfect disorder, and ran in every direction. About this time a sharp musketry fire commenced on our left, or old front, it being evident they were advancing another line through the cornfield. As we were of no more use in our present position, we went to the assistance of the other regiments of our brigade. We had so much changed the front that we moved by the left flank and filed left, connecting our left on the right of the Seventieth New York, and moved again down through the cornfield. We then pressed forward, driving the enemy before us, until the order was given to halt. I immediately deployed skirmishers forward through the field to an orchard. While moving through the cornfield, the enemy opened fire with grape and canister from two brass guns on our front, and shell from a battery on our right. It was by this fire that Col. Barlow fell, dangerously wounded. He was struck by a small piece of shell in the face, and a grape-shot in the groin. Thus far he had handled the two regiments in the most brave and skillful manner. As we had advanced further than the other regiments on our right and left, I was ordered to let the skirmishers remain and form in the open field on a line with Col. Brooks's regiment, which position we held until relieved by one of that brigade, when I marched them to the left of the line, and formed on a line with the Eighty-first Penn., and was not engaged again during the day.

I cannot speak in too high terms of the coolness and brave spirit with which both officers and men fought on that day. Col. Barlow on this, as on other occasions, displayed qualities for handling troops under fire which are not often met. Capt. Maze, Lieut. W. Keech, Lieut. Grannis and Lieut. T. W. Greig were noticed as behaving in the most excellent manner—also Dr. Tompkins, who followed the regiment upon the field and rendered prompt assistance to the wounded.

> Nelson A. Miles, Lieut. Col comdg. Sixty-first and Sixty-fourth New York Vols.''

Gen. Meagher's report of the operations of the Irish brigade does not place his men any nearer the enemy than they were when they were relieved by Barlow with the Sixty-first and Sixty-fourth New York.

In 1897 Capt. Lee Nutting of the Sixty-first N. Y., published an article in the New York " Sun," in which he modestly related the doings of Barlow's command at Antietam. His article called out the following:

To the Editor of the Sun—Sir:

" Without any dispargement of the Sixty-first New York comrades in our own Red Trefoil Division, allow me to suggest to your enthusiastic correspondent " L. N." that " there were others." Nor was the First Minnesota superimminently distinguished except at Gettysbusg. It was usually on provost duty. Gen. Walker had his preferences, but others of higher rank did not always agree with him. Sumner, Hancock, Richardson, Caldwell, Humphreys, and Symth thought the Irish brigade did pretty well. Their showing is quite respectable in Fox's " 300 Fighting Regiments." So did the enemy, and the opinion of the London Times correspondent from Fredericksburg is quoted in the history studied in our public schools (in Barnes's), while their charge at Antietam was specially mentioned by McClellan.

" By the way, the flags "captured" there by Barlow had already been marched over, with a lot of dead rebels, by the Eighty-eighth New York, who were too busy fighting to stop to pick them up. Miles was always a glorious fellow. Barlow did not like us, and once, under a mistake, joyfully exclaimed, "That d——d Irish brigade has broken at last!" to be corrected by Col. Smyth of the Sixty-ninth, who told him they had captured the enemy's works and he had come for further orders. (Signed) Irish Brigade.

The above makes quite a spicy newspaper article, but it does not read like history, and it Is Not history. Where and on what occasion did Francis C. Barlow ever manifest "joy" that the Irish, or any Union brigade "broke" when engaging the enemy! To my mind the statement is the equivalent of charging treason to one of the bravest fighters in the Union armies. And, according to this defender of the reputation of the Irish brigade, Barlow was thus filled with joy over what he believed to be the defeat of the Irish brigade "because he didn't like us." The above yarn is too idiotic to need replying to.

No sane person can believe a word of it. Except as every advance of troops may be said to be a "charge" the Irish brigade made no "charge" at Antietam, and McClellan in his report, dated Aug. 4th, 1863, covering the Antietam campaign, does not refer to any "charge" made by the Irish brigade in that battle. In this report (page 59, Series 1, Vol. 19) he says, "Meagher's brigade, advancing steadily, soon became engaged with the enemy posted to the left and in front of Roulett's house. It continued to advance under a heavy fire nearly to the crest of the hill overlooking Piper's house, the enemy being posted in a continuation of the sunken road and corn-field before referred to. Here the brave Irish brigade opened upon the enemy a terrific musketry fire. All of Gen. Sumner's corps was now engaged—Gen. Sedgwick on the right, Gen. French in the center, and Gen. Richardson on the left. The Irish brigade sustained its well earned reputation. After suffering terribly in officers and men, and strewing the ground with their enemies as they drove them back, their ammunition nearly exhausted, and their commander, Gen. Meagher, disabled from the fall of his horse shot under him, this brigade was ordered to give place to Gen. Caldwell's·"

Now, I say from personal observation that the Irish brigade was never farther in advance than the position it occupied when it was relieved by the Sixty-first and Sixty-fourth N. Y., that the Irish brigade did not, up to the time it was so relieved, pass over any ground that had been occupied by the enemy and on which they had left any of their battle flags. The battle flags captured by the Sixty-first and Sixty-fourth New York were taken from the sunken road. No one ever heard me say a word in derogation of the bravery of the Irish brigade. It was manifested at Antietam, and on a score of other battlefields. The glorious history of the second corps could not be written with its deeds left out. The Irish brigade stood in its tracks and took its terrible punishment at Antietam as heorically as did anything of Wellington's at Waterloo. Having said all this, the fact remains the brigade was NOT tactically well placed. Had it advanced to where the Sixty-first and Sixty-fourth later went, it would have done much greater execution, and with smaller loss to itself. The action of Barlow at Antietam proved beyond question his exceptional military ability.

On my way home after Gettysburg, I spent one night in the Citizens' hospital in Philadelphia. My cot was next to a Pennsylvanian's, who had lost a leg at Chancellorsville. When he learned I was of Barlow's regiment, he told me that about the finest sight he ever saw on the battlefield was see-ing Barlow lead his command into action at Antietam. He was where he had a full view of the display. The regiments were in line of battle, and he, with sabre in hand, was ahead of the line. Such is the plain fact, as all who were there can testify.

On the 19th of September, Gen. McClellan was informed that during the night Lee had pulled out, and placed the Potomac between him and us. The Army of Northern Virginia crossed the river at Shepardstown. Thus ended their proud invasion of Northern States.

We remained in our position for a number of days, bury-ing the dead, picking up the fragments, and getting ourselves together. The after view of a battle field is a horrible sight —wreck, ruin and devastation are on all sides; fences remov-ed, buildings more or less torn and demolished, wagons smashed, arms scattered about, artillery disabled, horses and mules piled up and swollen almost beyond recognition. All this shows the havoc of battle, but the sight that appals is the human dead. Dead, dying, and wounded in various ways. The spectator must callous his heart, or, if fairly human, he will be overwhelmed. There were places on this battlefield where the ground was literally strewn with those "beyond the fighting," swollen, grimy, unnatural, in all sorts of situations and positions. On the fence next to the cornfield, and just beyond the sunken road, were a number of Confederates hanging over the top rail, shot dead while trying to pass it. There they hung, like bundles of old clothes over a line.

"Gen. McClellan reported that he lost on the 16th and 17th 2,010 killed, 9,416 wounded and 1,043 missing—a total of 12,469. * * * * * McClellan reported that 2,700 of the

Confederate dead were counted and buried by his officers, and that a portion had been previously buried by their comrades." (The Antietam and Fredericksburg, Palfry, page 127.) Doubtless the killed, wounded and missing of the two armies would aggregate 25,000. The Second corps was the heaviest loser on the Union side, its casualties amounting to 5,138. (Walker 120)

On the 22d of September the army moved, the Second corps headed for Harpers Ferry, a distance of ten or twelve miles. We forded the Potomac just above the destroyed railroad bridge, and came to land opposite the ruins of the United States Armory. We went through the town and formed camp on Bolivar Heights. The time spent at this place was the soft kind of soldering. Supplies were abundant. Drill, guard, picket and police duties were light, and we all had a thoroughly good time. The scenery hereabouts is grand. Maryland, London and Boliver Heights come together, and from the tops of their heights to the river level is hundreds of feet. The passes worn by the Shenandoah and Potomac are through the solid rock and the gorges are very deep and rugged.

Our picket line was a mile or two out toward Charlestown. While on one of these picketing details, while the first relief was on, Frank Garland suggested that, if possible, we slip through the line, go to the front and see if we couln't pick up something good to eat. We succeeded in passing the pickets and pointed for a farm house a half mile ahead. For a time no one responded to our knocks and helloes. At last a plump, red cheeked modest girl, of perhaps sixteen, appeared. We enquired for apples and told her if she would fill our haversacks, we would be glad to pay for them. She took them and soon returned with them filled with eatable apples. We paid her the price charged and started back. We admitted to one another that it was not a prudent act and would go hard with us if we should be picked up. On our way back Garland glanced to the left, and said, " There's reb cavalry!" I looked, and there, perhaps an eighth of a mile away, was a squad of horsemen, coming on a canter toward us. We were near a substantial rail fence on the right, and for it we sprang with all our powers. We went over it like circus performers, and put in our best strides for our line. I think it was Garland that first discovered that the "men on horseback" were negro farm hands. They had seen our lively retreat and accurately interpreted the cause, and they were with their mouths open as wide as their jaws would admit, haw-hawing near the point of splitting. On this discovery we slowed down, and sauntered toward our picket line as unconcerned as possible, but the pickets had seen the performance, and at first had been misled as we were. As we came in we proposed to go straight to the reserve where the detail from our regiment was. The officer in charge refused this and sent us under a guard of two men and a corporal to headquarters. We steered the corporal to the shelter tent of Capt. Bull and explained the situation to him. He took it in, and, with a large assumption of military dignity, informed the guard that he would relieve them of any further duty in the matter, and they could go back to the front. Garland and I were glad to divide our apples with Bull and the others who knew of our adventure. It was one of the worst scares I had in the service, and cured me of any attempt at foraging outside the lines.

Gen. Walker says, "The only episode which interruped the pleasant monotone of rest and equipment, after the fatigues of the Manassas and Antietam campaigns, was a reconnoissance conducted by Gen. Hancock with the first division Oct. 16th down the valley to Charlestown, with the view to discovering whether the enemy were there in force." We met a battery supported by cavalry, which fell back as we advanced. The captain of this battery was B. H. Smith, Jr. and was wounded. We found him in a house at Charlestown with a foot amputated. We spent the night in Charlestown, and while there many of the boys visited the tree where John Brown had his taking off Dec. 2, 1859.

On the 25th of October, I wrote a letter home from which I quote, "The whole regiment cannot turn out over 50 or 60 charter members. I will give you a list of Co. "C," which left Hamilton but little over one year ago full of hope and great expectation. Today we have present Capt. Broady, broken in mind and body by hardship and disease; Serg. Isaac Plumb, well and in good spirits; Serg. C. A. Fuller, ditto; Serg. D. W. Skinner, suffering from old wound, and who will be discharged; Portner E. Whitney, pioneer, good soldier; George Jacobs, private, cooking for the company; Junuis Gaskell, sick most of the time; Charles Richards, paroled prisoner, sees no duty; Freeman Allen has a bad leg; Rufus Rundell, in quartermaster's department—always has been; John Boardman, drummer. Where are the other 80? Some 10 or 11 killed, three times that number wounded, 10 dead of disease, 8 or 10 discharged, and the remainder sick in hospitals. Ike and myself are the only ones of that ninety odd, who have been in every engagement with the regiment, and he was not carrying a gun at Fair Oaks. Lieut. Keech is the only line officer who has been in all the regiment's battles. This may seem incredible, but it is nevertheless true—some would miss this battle and some that, and so, but one has missed none."

On the 29th of October, 1862, our army broke camp and moved in the direction of Warrenton, which place we reached on the 11th of November. In making this march the Sixty-first skirmished over the mountains at Snecker's Gap, driving back a body of calvary that was observing, if not holding this position. From the ridge of the mountain we had a view that in my judgment could not be equaled in Europe.

While the army was at Warrenton the order came removing McClellan and appointing Burnside. For one I was glad of any change—it seemed to be that no one could be more inefficient than McClellan. I remember so expressing myself which was not a popular notion. One old Irishman of Co. A, turned on me in hot anger, and asked, "Why do you say that? What do you know about war, you little damned pie eater!"

In a few days we started out and reached Falmouth, a hamlet nearly opposite Fredericksburg on the Rappahannock river on the 17th of November. There were but a handful of rebels on the other side of the river. There was no attempt to ford it, and we went into camp, while Lee's army soon concentrated about Fredericksburg. Our camp was located in the woods, which we partially cleared, converting the timber into walls for our huts, which we covered with our shelter tent canvass. In a few days we had comfortable quarters. Part of the time the weather was quite cold. Snow was on the ground, and the brook that ran near by was more or less covered with ice. I remember going down to this brook one Sunday morning with Portner E. Whitney. We took off our clothing and had a bath in that ice cold water. We were in this camp for several weeks, and in it had first rate good times. Near to us was a Pennsylvania regiment, (I forget the number) in which a "revival of religion" prevailed. Meetings were held continuously and it was reported that many were converted. I think this regiment suffered severely in the great slaughter of the 13th of December.

Quite early in December indications multiplied that a move. ment was contemplated. Three days rations were ordered to be kept constantly in the haversacks. Charles Lowell, our hospital steward, told me that the surgeons had received orders to put in good condition the operating instruments, and frequent inspections made sure that enough ammunition was in the boxes.

On Thursday, Dec. 11th, at 4 a. m., reveille beat, after roll call the men were told that they must be ready to break camp on short notice. At 6 a. m. the regiment formed on the color line, ready to move. While we were thus waiting, I was smoking my briarwood pipe, and, at what I supposed was the end of the smoke, I threw out the ashes and put the pipe in my breeches pocket. In a short time I was conscious of a change of temperature in that locality, and hastily brought to view the pocket and pipe. Doubtless some of the fire remained in the bowl, which got out and set fire to that part of my clothing. I had no trouble in extinguishing this ignition, but the pocket was gone and my leg had a raw spot.

At this time the Army of the Potomac was organized in three grand divisions as follows: Right Grand Division, Sumner's, embracing the Second and Ninth corps; Center Grand Division, Hooker's, Third and Fifth corps; Left Grand Division, Sixth and First corps. Gen. D. N. Couch commanded the Second corps; Hancock the First Division, and Caldwell the First brigade of the corps.

While in this camp that we were about to leave I had the honor to be the object to which a brief utterance was directed by Gen. Hancock. I was then a sergeant, and had been ordered to brigade headquarters with a squad of men for guard duty. On the day in question, Gen. Sumner reviewed his Grand Division. After the guard had got to its place, one of Caldwell's staff came to me and said, " When the general comes along you will fall in your guard and present arms." I had some eight or ten men with me, and told those not on duty to be on hand to fall in when so ordered. Presently I heard a horse coming down the road on a sharp gallop, and soon saw that it was Gen. Hancock with a single orderly. Evidently he was not on the lookout for a little guard to salute him, but I fell in the men as briskly as possible. The general noticed what I was doing, and had to wait a moment for the guard to present arms, which it did all right. Hancock returned the compliment, and then said to me, " If you want to salute, sir! you must be a 'damned sight quicker' than this!" If I had dared to, I would have answered, " Don't you worry yourself, Winfield Scotty, I don't want to salute you, and wouldn't now, if I had not been ordered to."

Of course I kept my mouth shut. It would have been bad policy to have expressed my sentiments.

As I have stated, shortly after 6 a. m. our column started We made a roundabout march of a few miles and finally halted, under cover of high ground, nearly opposite the city of Fredericksburg. All this day a furious cannonade was maintained by our side, and from big guns mounted on the crest back of the river. The effort was to clean the enemy out from the neighborhood of the river bank, so that we could lay our pontoon bridges. This was not successful, and in the attempt to do this work our men were picked off, so that it was found to be impracticable. At length the Seventh Mich. and the 89th N. Y. were rushed into the poonton boats and rowed and poled over. Once on the other shore they drove away the sharpshooters, and the bridge at our front was then laid. We remained that night on the Falmouth side of the river. The next forenoon the Second corps crossed the river. Our division was marched along the side of the river, to the lower end of the city, and then we stacked arms.

Some of our men inspected the near by houses on their own motion, and from one they brought out a jar of fresh tried lard. I had a chance at it and spread it on my hard tack, as I would butter at home. I have had my share of good butter and love it, but I never tasted bread greasing equal to that new lard.

Towards night we were marched back to the site of the railroad bridge, and billited in the grist mill near said bridge. One of our men procured a duck, I was let into the mess, and in some way we cooked and disposed of it before rolling up in our blankets for a good night's rest. We turned out early the next morning, (the disastrous 13th) and after breakfast, lead by Col. Miles, we went through the city to the last street. Here our little regiment was deployed as a sort of picket line. To the front half or three-quarters of a mile ran the top of a line of hills, parallel to our street. Not so much as the crack of a pistol had broken the silence of the morning. We lounged about, viewed from between the houses the supposed location of the enemy, went into the houses next to where we were posted, and helped ourselves. Not a soldier in gray was to be seen, save here and there a sentry watching from the top of their earth works. One of our boys was inspecting the contents of the house of a doctor, I forget his name. Presently he called to me and inquired if I didn't want some books. I said "Yes." He tossed me from the window a fine volume of Byron's poems, and the two volumes of Dr. Kane's Arctic Explorations. I sat on the curbing looking over this plunder, when, all at once, a number of big guns went off, and very soon thereafter shot and shell came thundering through the houses, across our street, and into the houses behind us. I hurriedly dropped my spoils, and made quick tracks for the other side of the street, where there was, perhaps, better protection. This artillery outburst was due to the appearance of our troops, moving out of the city and towards the strong position of the enemy.

In a few minutes Col. Miles assembled the Sixty-first and marched it back into the next street, where we stood in line ready for the word "Go!" In this position nothing could be seen, but the shots and shells of our adversaries came thick and dangerously near, though none were to my knowledge effective. While we were here I noticed one of our recruits, a German, who was literally unnerved by fear. His countenance was distorted by terror, and he was shaking in every limb. I think it was impossible for him to march. I do not remember ever seeing him after that time. For myself I confess that I never exerted more will power to make my legs move in the right direction than just here. Without pretending to have military judgment, as I viewed the intrenched position of the Confederates, I said to myself, "we will fail to carry those heights."

At length the order came to move, and the head of our column started for the street that led to Marye's Hill. Turning into it we advanced rapidly. My recollection is, that as the road leaves the city, it makes a slight curve, and as we came to that spot the whole view was opened up to us. I know the road was littered with some dead, and cast off blankets and knapsacks. For a ways the road slightly descends, and then you come to a considerable stream of some sort, it may be a waste weir, from the Falmouth dam. This stream was bridged, and a part, if not all, of the flooring of it had been removed. I remember we, partially at least, crossed on the stringers. At this point the enemy concentrated a hot artillery fire. I think the Sixty-first got over without much damage, but the head of the regiment following took in several shells that caused heavy loss. We pressed forward to a point part way up the hill to the front, when the order was given "On the right, by file into line!" This deployed us in line of battle to the left of the road we had been advancing on. The rise of ground was sufficient to protect us from the enemy, while we were thus forming. Hancock rode his horse up and down the line between us and the foe.

While we stood here, one of the ghastly sights of war was almost under my feet. A soldier lay nearly where I ought to have stood. A shell had gone through his body, and in its passage had set fire to his clothing, and there his corpse lay slowly cooking. There was no time to do anything.

At least one line of battle had preceded us, and, I suppose, had been used up. Now the order came for us to advance, which we did, probably in brigade line of battle. I cannot say how many regiments there were in it. I know we advanced till within musket range of the rebel rifle pits, when we were halted and ordered to lie down. We did not fire, but the enemy did from their pits and they picked off some of our men. After a short time we were ordered to stand up. I then noticed that sergeant Israel O. Foote of my company was lying on the ground wounded, and evidently in pain. Our column was right faced and put in motion. We advanced parallel to the rebel line, and under their fire. We soon came to the road. Here there was a house or two, and the building, or buildings, had some soldiers in it, or them. We crossed the road—the Sixty-first under Miles did—and brought up in a yard or garden patch that had a high tight board fence on two sides of it. Here we were directed to lie down. The fence hid the enemy from our sight, but the distance to their nearest line of rifle pits was short. Occasional projectiles from cannon and muskets came our way, so that most of us were willing to hug the ground.

George Joyce of Co. C was with the regiment, just returned from hospital partially recovered from a wound received at Malvern Hill. Joyce was a unique character, small of stature, illiterate, an adroit forager, and, if you didn't know him, you might take him for a mere braggadocio. But such was not the case. He was destitute of fear, or, if he ever experienced the sensation, he overcame it. At Glendale the Colonel ordered the line forward. A soldier said " We will follow the colors." Joyce was a private, and how he happened to have them I do not know, but he did, and he marched forward, brought the staff down with a bang and said, " There's your colors, come up to them !" The line moved up, and Barlow made him orderly sergeant of (I think) Co. F then and there. Joyce was back with a stiff arm, so that he could not carry a gun, but while most of us were hugging the ground, he stood up and worked his jaw. He said, " Lie low boys. "I'll let you know if anything happens." And so he was on the watch. Presently a solid shot came his way. It passed so near his foot, that, while it made no visible abrasion, his foot began to swell so that he had to cut his boot off, and he had to hobble back.

It was said at the time that Col. Miles, satisfied that the only thing to do to amount to anything, was to make a rush and take this first picket line, had sent back his conclusion, and requested permission to charge the line with his regiment. About this time an accommodating rebel bullet cut his throat, letting out a liberal quantity of fresh bright blood. This so put him *hors de combat* that he had to leave the field, somewhat to the longevity account of the Sixty-firsters there present. So we continued in this lowly attitude till after Hooker's men made another vain assault over the ground we had occupied. Then, toward sundown, we were withdrawn, and marched back into the city, and took up our quarters for the night in the same grist mill we occupied the night before.

So far as we could see, nothing was done the next day, Sunday. But little, if any, fighting was had on Monday. After dark Monday evening our regiment, under command, I think of Capt. Kettle, was marched back as far to the front as we had occupied Saturday, but to the right. Here we were placed in rifle pits that would hold half a dozen each. There was a space of eight or ten feet between each pit. Here we were very close to the enemy—we could hear their movements, and they ours. I should think it was as late as 3 o'clock a. m. of Tuesday when we were withdrawn, and silently made our way to the city, and through it, and to the pontoon bridge we crossed the Friday before. We were nearly the last to cross. Shortly afterward the bridge was taken up, and the Rappahannock again flowed between the hostile camps.

In this battle the only original members of Co. C present with the company were Sergt. I. O. Foote, killed ; Geo. Jacobs and myself. Isaac Plumb had been commissioned and transferred to another company and Whitney was with the pioneers.

We marched directly to our old camp. We found things as we left them, and we proceeded, as far as we could with what was on hand, to restore the camp to the condition it was in before we broke it on the 12th.   Many of the men had disposed of shelter tents and blankets during the worthless movement, so that some of the huts had no covering.   The next day Gen. Sumner rode up to our camp and had some talk with the men.   He asked why some of the huts were not covered with canvass.   We said, "We dumped them when we went into the fight."   He replied, "You should have stuck to your tents and blankets!"   This was the last time I saw the old man.   He left the army in January, 1863, and died in bed about three months later at his home in Syracuse, N. Y.   He was a great Corps Commander.

Burnside's next *fiasco* was called his "stuck in the mud" campaign.   In this case he was to cross the river to the right about where Hooker did four months later.   In this movement the centre and left broke camp while Sumner's Grand Division remained to take care of the enemy's right at Fredericksburg.   A terrible storm ended the movement almost before it was begun, and we remained comfortable in camp.

Shortly after this Burnside resigned, and Gen. Joseph Hooker was appointed Commander of the Army of the Potomac.   Hooker had been named "Fighting Joe Hooker."   As a rule I think, the men were pleased with the change.

On the 13th of February, 1863, the 61st and the 64th broke camp and moved a few miles to the left, and went into the camp lately occupied by the 27th New Jersey, a regiment of Burnside's old corps, which went with him when he left the Army of the Potomac.   The Grand Division formation was abandoned when Hooker took command, and the former corps organization re-adopted.   Our new camp was delightfully situated.   It fronted about twenty rods back from the edge of the high bluff, which was, perhaps, eighty rods back from the edge of the river.   We were below, but in plain view of Fredericksburg.   The New Jerseyites had made for themselves better quarters than I had ever occupied, and we "entered into their labors."   I never enjoyed soldiering more than during the weeks we were in this place.   Much of the time the weather was good, and we drilled, did picket duty, and got in readiness for the next grapple.

On the 21st of February I received notice that I had been

commissioned Second Lieutenant of Co. C. It was at the time, next to nothing in the field. It did not have over two privates in the ranks, with a sergeant, a drummer and a pioneer. In place of creating new regiments, when the last call was filled, the men should have been sent to the old regiments in the field.

On the 16th of March I was officer of the day for our camp, and, of course, was up and about at all hours of that day and the next night. During the forepart of this service nothing occurred to make it in any way notable, so far as I was concerned, but about 3 o'clock in the morning of the next day, I heard, a considerable distance to the right, a yelling and cheering, and a general "whoopering up" that I couldn't account for. I hurried to Col. Miles's tent and reported. He directed me to send out a couple of men to find out. In due time they came back and reported that the Irish Brigade were celebrating "St. Patrick's Day in the Morning." The boys with the green flag had a great day of it, in which several barrels of commissary were made dry.

On the 14th of April I wrote home that, probably, the Army would move in a few days. Eight days rations were distributed to the men—five were to be stored in the knapsacks and three in the haversacks. Extra baggage was packed and sent to the rear.

On this day Lieut. Plumb started for home on a ten days leave of absence. He returned and was in his place before the movement came. It was over a year since I had seen home and I had an application in for a like leave, but the situation prevented its issue until after the next great defeat. The 29th of April we broke camp and were ready to join our brigade at a moment's notice. We did not start till early the next day. During these hours I had a bilious attack, and was sick enough to die, but the tents were all down, and there was no chance to baby me. I groaned and grunted till about the time the regiment started, and then *I had* to move or be left behind. I well remember how I staggered in my attempt to march, but I kept at it, and before night was pretty well. I had a number of such experiences, so that, I conclude, if the screws were more frequently put to people in civil life, there would be many cases of like cures.

We advanced but a few miles and camped. The next day we spent some time in making corduroy road, and advanced but a few miles. April 30th we advanced to the vicinity of the river (Rappahannock) and stacked arms in a piece of woods. If I remember correctly it was here and then that our corps badges were issued. Ours was the trefoil, and our division's red. The colors for all corps were : first division, red ; second division, white ; third division, blue. Couch was in command of the second Corps. Hancock was still our division general, and Caldwell our brigade general. In this place I saw Hancock and Caldwell ride by. Hancock was mad about something, and he was shaking his fist under Caldwell's nose, and God-daming him at the top of his capacity. Hancock was a brave and capable general, but he was demonstratively passionate, and vilely abusive with his tongue. Junius Gaskell of my Company was for months his private orderly, and he saw the polish and the rough of him. Gaskell has told me that he would get mad at his own brother, who was assistant adjutant general of the division, and blaspheme at him and call him the conventional name a man uses, when he wants to say a mean thing of the other fellow based on the alleged status of his mother.

Towards sundown we were put in motion, making our way to the river's edge, and crossed it on a well-laid pontoon. We ate our supper on the other side of the river, and then advanced a few miles into the country, and halted for the night along side an open piece of woods, not far from the Chancellorsville house. We went into this piece of woods to spread our blankets to bivouac for the night. Our cavalry had been on this ground before, and they had responded affirmatively to the calls of nature, so that we soon discovered we were treading on mounds not as large, but as soft, as the one into which Peter Stuyvesant fell, according to the narrative of Irving. I remember, after spreading my own blanket, that my hand dropped down outside of it, and went slap into one of those mounds. I further remember that I was not the only Sixty-firster that imprecated in strong Saxon. But there we were, and there we lay till sunrise. We learned that the day before a lively skirmish had been fought here, in which one of our Colonels was killed.

Friday, May 1st, about 11 a. m., the artillery became engaged. Before long the Sixty-first N. Y., and the Hundred and Forty-eight Pennsylvania were ordered forward, and we went to the front and right of what I suppose became our line. We worked our way through a piece of scrub pine that was almost impervious, having passed this obstruction, we were in open ground, and we advanced, I think, in skirmish line formation. It was not long before we met Mr. Johnny Reb., and in such force that we fell back at a lively pace, and worked our way through the scrub I have spoken of. We emerged into a large open field where there were a good many troops. By this time the shells of the enemy were making it interesting for us. Hancock was present, and rushed matters in his energetic way to get his men deployed where he wanted them. In due time we were placed in the woods not far from the clearing. We had not more than got into position when these woods were shelled. We were ordered to lie down, and the order was well observed. It seemed to me that I was never under such a raking fire, the noise was fearful, and the amputated tree limbs came down on us like snow flakes in a Winter's squall. So far as I know, no one was seriously hurt in this terrifying bombardment. After it ceased we moved to another position in the woods, stacked arms, and there spent the night, or till towards morning of the Second, (Saturday.)

Before it was fairly light, we were put in motion and a good deal of time was spent to satisfactorily locate us. As I understand it, we were placed in sight of, and to the left of the Chancellorsville House. We at once stacked arms. A line for rifle pits was run out, and one set of men began to intrench, while another set, with axes, were in front slashing down the timber—falling it to the front, and tangling it, so that it was impossible to rapidly work through it. Before night we had seemingly an impregnable line. It could not have been carried by infantry from the front. Artillery might have battered down our defences, or infantry might have turned it, but we hoped that the Confederates would see fit to attack our line with infantry from the front. Gen. Howard, with the Eleventh Corps, was on the right of our line.

He had been duly notified during the day that there was a movement of Rebel troops towards his end of the line. No doubt he was a brave man and believed he could repel any attack that might be made on him, but where the great issues of a battle are at stake, a commander has no business to take needless chances, and, when he can, he should put his men under cover as effectually as may be, so that he can accomplish his purpose with as little loss of limb and life as possible. If, as soon as the Eleventh Corps was located they had gone to work cutting the timber to the front and intrenching, as Hancock's men did, Jackson would have met a bloody repulse, and Chancellorsville would have been our victory. Instead of that, his guns were stacked, his men were lounging about, and absolutely without protection. (Doubleday's Chancellorsville and Gettysburg, page 26 and following.) Jackson struck him with a column of 26,000 men about 6 p. m., and stampeded his force as if they had been ewe lambs. After reading many different accounts of this battle, I am fully persuaded that Howard inexcusably, if not criminally, blundered on this occasion. In regular course of time the "stampedees," if I may use the word, came across the country and struck our line. They were entirely in favor of continuing on, but we protested against it, and told them they would run right into the rebel lines. Some were still bound to go, when the argument of the bayonet converted them to our idea, and they camped down in our rear. Sunday, the 3d, found us in the same place, standing guns in hand behind our breastworks. The fighting to our right was heavy and continuous. About 11 a. m. it was evident the Rebels had forced our position. We saw our men streaming back, in a brief time the enemy had posted artillery that raked our line. It was no longer tenable, and we were ordered to fall back on the double quick. As we did so, we were under heavy artillery fire. We passed near the Chancellor House, which was at the time, I believe, on fire. We halted about one-fourth of a mile to the rear, and there formed line of battle in the edge of the woods. While we were waiting, a number of high class women were located close to us. I was told at the time they were the occupants of the Chancellor House, then burning to the ground. I remember writing home and telling my people that these women were interesting to look at, and that their features expressed fear and hate. In a little time they were marched off, and the Sixty-first with a part, if not all of the brigade, were advanced, I should think, at right angles with the position held by us for two days. We soon entered a piece of woods and advanced in line of battle through it. As we came near to the clearing beyond, we saw the rifle pits of the enemy, and we met at our part of the line quite a brisk fire, but on the right it was exceedingly severe. One company of the 148th Pa. lost more than half its men. Then our line fell back to the place from which we had advanced, and we at once began another set of entrenchments. In a few hours time we had again defences that we would have been delighted to see assaulted by our friends, the enemy.

In order to keep us from going to seed the Rebels would occasionally send over a shell, or solid shot, and they had the true range very well. I remember while such a practice was under way, and we were on our bellies back from the breastworks some three rods, so that we might not be hurt by the top log if it should be hit by a ball or shell, a large solid shot came hurtling over, just above the top of our works, and plunged into the ground close to the feet of a sandy-haired Irishman by the name of Flarity. I think I was looking that way at the moment. Flarity felt the sweep of the wind as the shot went over him ; he raised up sufficiently to see where it had gone into the ground, and said, " Whist, ye divil ! was yee's *intinded* for me ? " Those who saw the effect of the shot and heard Flarity had a loud smile.

We were not attacked on Monday, though during the day Lieut-Col. Broady called the officers around him and informed them in his Swedish brogue, that it was anticipated that the enemy would charge our position, which we were to hold as long as there was a man left of us, and that if we should give way and fall back we would be fired into by our men, who held a second and third line. This was delightful information, and made us feel very jolly—" over the left ? " but I am satisfied there was not a man in the crowd that would have gone back if the chance had been offered. The attack did not come, and during the night we began the backward march again, which had come to be almost a matter of course. Hooker had twice as many men as Lee, and the movement seemed to open encouragingly. While Doubleday and Walker and Alden do not in so many words say that Hooker was drunk, I think that is the clear inference. If he was, shooting would be too good for him, he ought to have been burned at the stake.

Saturday morning, the second day of May, Col. Miles was put in command of the picket line to our front. His own regiment was not in this advance line, but was in the first main line behind the works that I have mentioned. Our Colonel here made a great reputation for himself. I quote from Swinton, "Amid much that is dastardly at Chancellorsville, the conduct of this young, but gallant and skillful officer, shines forth with a brilliant lustre." Walker says of him, "So delighted was Hancock at the splendid behavior of his skirmish line that, after one repulse of the enemy, he exclaimed, 'Capt. Parker, ride down and tell Col. Miles he's worth his weight in gold!'" While Couch, turning to the Major-Generals who commanded his two divisions, said, in his quiet but emphatic way, "I tell you what it is, gentlemen, I shall not be surprised to find myself, some day serving under that young man." Shortly after he was dangerously wounded through the body. Walker says (page 240) "Hancock strengthens the skirmish line held by Miles, and instructs that officer not to yield one foot, except on actual necessity; and well is that trust discharged. The troops under Miles's command consist of the 61st, 64th and 66th New York, with detachments from the 53d Pa, 2d Delaware, and 146th, 145th and 148th Pa. and 27th Conn." The historian of the Second Corps is in error when he writes that the 61st was placed on the skirmish line. As I have before stated, it remained behind the works it built, until the position was enfiladed by the enemy's artillery, and then it, with the rest of that line, fell back.

He is again in error when he says, (page 244) speaking of the disaster of the 3d, "Hancock's division was no longer intact. Caldwell, with the 61st, 52d and 57th N. Y., and four companies of the 148th Pa., had, at a sudden call, marched to the United

States Ford road, with a view to the anticipated breaking through of the enemy from the right and rear." Unless the movement above described is the one made through the wood, in which the 148th Pa. suffered so severely.

During Monday night and Tuesday morning we started back, and after daylight Tuesday, the 5th of May, we "*got back on our side of the Rappahannock.*" Before night we were again on our camp ground of the December before.

May 11th I received a fifteen days leave of absence, for which I had applied before the late movement. Those granted prior to the move had been but for ten days. Probably the extra five days was in the nature of a premium for the delay caused by the campaign, and the service in it. I made the most of this time, and was so feasted at home that I started back several pounds heavier than when I left. I did not desire to be away long. At the end of the leave I was anxious to be again with the boys. At this time I was tenting with Nutting and Collins. Nutting came down with typhoid fever. He was sent to hospital, and returned in the Fall.

While in this camp, June 1st, 1863, the First Brigade of the First Division, fell in and passed in review by quite a body of officers, including Hancock, Howard and Barlow. Gen. Howard made appropriate remarks to the remnants of the 5th N. H., 81st Pa., 64th and 61st N. Y., which he commanded in the battle of Fair Oaks that day, the year before. But a small fraction of the men he commanded that day at 7 a. m. were present to hear his words. He said we were in this great strife to win, and we would fight it to a finish, and we applauded his sentiments by lusty cheers. After this we returned to our quarters. Barlow appeared and gave us a chance to grasp his hand. I am sure this great soldier always had a special affection for the men of the 61st N. Y. He had their entire confidence. Unquestionably they obeyed his orders, first, perhaps, because they didn't dare do otherwise, and, second, because they trusted his judgment and ability to perform what he set out to do.

Now everything indicated a move at short notice. Sunday, the 14th of June, the Confederates shot off their big guns on the heights of Fredericksburg. I think our people crossed the river on a reconnaissance. At 8 p. m. the Second Corps moved, marched four miles and halted for the night. Monday, the 15th, we passed Stafford Court House. Tuesday, the 16th, the march took us beyond Dumfries' Court House. This day was excessively hot, and it was stated that quite a number of the Second Corps died of sunstroke. Lieut. Elmore was striken down by it. He lay on the ground almost motionless—was quite out of his head and talked crazy. He was put into an ambulance, and sent to hospital.

Wednesday, the 17th, at the close of the day, we halted at Pope's Run on the Orange & Alexandria R. R. Thursday, the 18th, no move was made, except to change camp. In the afternoon of Friday (the 19th) we moved and halted in the evening at Centreville, the place we had been in about nine months before. Saturday about noon we left Centreville for Thoroughfare Gap. We passed over the two Bull Run battlefields, which were fought about a year apart. On the field of 1861 the dead had been buried with the least expenditure of labor. I should say the bodies had been laid close together, and a thin coat of earth thrown over them. As the bodies decayed, the crust fell in exposing in part the skeletons. Some of our men extracted teeth from the grinning skulls as they lay thus exposed to view. On the field of 1862 from one mound a hand stuck out. The flesh instead of rotting off had dried down, and there it was like a piece of dirty marble. Such sights are not refreshing to men going forward in search of a new battlefield. Thoroughfare Gap was reached during the night. We remained in this place until noon of Thursday, the 25th, when we moved, the enemy following us up quite sharply with artillery.

After dark we camped at Gum Spring. It had rained all day. I was placed in charge of the picket line that night, and visited the posts wet to the skin. In the morning a young and innocent calf was sporting in the field we occupied. Some of our wickedest men ended the life of that calf skinned it, and gave me a chunk. I expected to have an unusually good meal out of it. No time was found to cook this meat until we halted at Edward's Ferry on the Potomac, where we expected to spend the night. Collins and I proposed to have a great meal out of our piece of veal. Our man " Robert " fried it in the stew pan, which was the half of a canteen, and brought it on smoking hot. The experiment of trying to eat it disclosed the fact that it was " deeken veal " and very "*stringy*," I think the Spanish war soldiers would have called it. We discarded it and went back to "salt hoss."

That night we crossed the Potomac on a pontoon, and were again in "My Maryland." The performances this night were such as to justify vocal daming on the part of a very good Christian. The men were tired, but they were marched and counter-marched, and halted and started, and placed and unplaced, until it was fair to conclude that someone was drunk. At last the person directing the column got his bearings and we proceeded. We were plodding along a road in which there was on the right hand side a ditch about two feet deep. Having been up and awake all of the night before, I was fearfully sleepy and hardly able to drag myself along. All at once I went into this ditch, and struck full length. In its bottom there was about two inches of mud, thick enough to encase me. By the time I had pawed out, I could not, if laid out, have been distinguished from a mud sill; but I was too near gone to speak bad words, and so went on in silence, weighing five pounds more than before my descent. Before long we halted and bivouaced for the night. The next morning, the 27th, our regiment started about 10 o'clock, and was thrown out as an advance guard to our baggage train. Along the line of this march there were numerous wild black cherry trees. They were loaded with ripe fruit, and we ate our fill. I think we covered 25 miles this day, and went into camp near Frederick City. We were over this same ground less than a year before, and everything looked as it then did.

Sunday, the 28th, we moved up, and camped just before crossing the Monocacy. We spent the day very comfortably, and went to bed by rolling up in our blankets, when an order came to "fall in." This we did of course, but wished it had been otherwise. We marched about two miles, and were posted to guard a ford of the Monocacy. We had with us a section of artillery.

Monday, the 29th, we made a march of over thirty-two miles. We halted for the night some miles beyond Union-town, at about 10 p. m. I know I was so completely tired out, that, as soon as arms were stacked, I stretched out without unrolling my blankets, and I knew nothing till the next morning, when I was awakened by the sun shining into my eyes. I was so stiff that it took some time to get on to my legs, but, after moving about for a while, I was all right.

Tuesday, the 30th, we remained in camp, many straggled in the march of the day before, and during this day most of them came up. Wednesday, July 1st, we started out, none of us knowing for where. We heard no sound of battle that day. No doubt the lay of the land shut off the thunder of the guns. A rumor soon became current that a fight was in progress, and that Gen. Reynolds had been killed. We marched through a little village, perhaps it was Taneytown. Our signalers were up in the steeple of a church on the street we were passing through, and their flags were we-wawing at a great rate. Before long the ambulance containing the corpse of Reynolds passed us. We halted for the night. After sundown our brigade, and probably the division, were in line of battle. As soon as arms were stacked, we went to a rail fence, took down the rails, brought them to our line, and, before going to bed—i. e., spreading our blankets on the ground—we had staked up those rails and banked earth against them so that they would have served quite a purpose as breastworks. By this time lines of camp fires were burning as far as we could see, indicating that the army was massed here, or the ruse was worked to make the enemy think so.

Thursday, the 2d, we were quietly ordered to turn out. Breakfast was eaten, the guns and ammunition were inspected, and by six or seven o'clock we were in motion. On the march I remember we went through a small piece of open timber, where our doctors were posted, and as we went by we shook hands with them, and exchanged little pleasantries. I remember saying to them, "We'll see you again later." I tried to say this with a jaunty air, but down in my shoes I did not feel a bit jaunty. I think we all felt that this should be a death grapple, and, if Lee went further north, it ought to be over the played out ranks of this army. We continued our march and halted in a large open field to the left of the village of Gettysburg. Our brigade was massed, and commanded by Col. Edward E. Cross of the 5th N. H.

We remained in this place during the long hours of the

day. There was no noise, save occasionally slight picket firing, but it was not the silence of assured quiet. It was the painful waiting before the descent of the certain cyclone.

Our regiments were so small that, except in the case of the 148th Pennsylvania, each regiment made a single line. I think the 148th was divided into two battalions. The 61st had about 90 muskets. While waiting for something to "turn up" Col. Cross came up, and after a little said, "Boys, you know what's before you. Give 'em hell!" and some of us said "We will, Colonel!" After a time "the ball opened" on our left. A determined attack was made on Sickel's position. He could not hold it, and re-enforcements were sent to him. I do not remember seeing the 5th N. H. move away but Col. Broady says it was detached before the brigade started. I think it was between 5 and 6 o'clock when our orders came, and we were ready. It was preferable to advance into action, rather than to wait in expectation of the order to move. The direction we were to take was to the front and left. There was no time to countermarch so as to bring the men right in front, so we simply left faced and started. The 61st, since the withdrawal of the 5th N. H. was the right regiment. We advanced in this manner, the brigade in a chunck, until we struck a cross road. In this road we deployed by filing right and advancing until the regiments were deployed, then we left faced. This undoubled us, and we stood in line of battle, officers and sergeants in front of the rear rank in front. In front of us across the road was a wheatfield, which was bounded by a fence. We were ordered forward; we scaled the fence and advanced into this wheatfield in line of battle, as I have stated. Finally we were halted, markers were thrown out, and we lined up. The 61st N. Y. was the right of our brigade line. I am not sure what regiment was to our right. It is my recollection that no regiment was in close contact with us. As soon as the alignment was perfected, the officers and file closers passed through the ranks and got in rear of the men. Up to this time not a confederate had been seen in our front.

At the further edge of this wheatfield there were the rem-

nants of a stone wall and scattering trees and brush, which
made a natural line for the opposing force to form behind.
As soon as I got into my place I kept my eyes to the front,
and in a few seconds I saw first one or two men come toward
us on a run, and throw themselves down behind this partial
stone wall. But a brief time passed when a solid line of
men in gray appeared and placed themselves as had the first
comers. At once, and without any ordering, the firing
opened by both sides. It was slightly descending from where
we stood to the position of the enemy. I think their location was the best, independent of the protection afforded by
the old wall. It was a case of give and take. As a rule our
men behaved splendidly ; with a single exception I saw no
flinching or dodging. I saw a certain second lieutenant
doubling himself together so as to bring his head below the
line of the heads of the men in front of him. Capt. Keech
saw his posture and came up to him and said, "Stand up !"
What are you crouching for ?" The fellow replied, "I'm not
crouching." Keech replied, "Yes, you are !" and he hit him
across his humped-up back a sharp rap that made him grunt,
and said, "Stand up like a man !" In battle the tendency is
almost universal for the men to work out of a good line into
clumps. The men of natural daring will rather crowd to the
front, and those cast in more timid or retiring molds will
almost automatically edge back and slip in behind. Hence
the necessity of not alone commissioned officers in the rear to
keep the men out in two ranks, but sergeants as well. I
think I have stated that there were less than one hundred
men present with the regiment. For the less than ninety
muskets in the ranks we had a number of commissioned officers. More than was needed. We had officers enough in
our regiment in this great battle to have commanded three
hundred men, and it is a standing proof of the gross ignorance, or the villainy of the New York government that such
was the case. In the early part of the day I remarked to a
number of the men near by that when some one of them was
knocked out I was going to take his musket and get into the
firing line. We were in this wheatfield and the grain stood
almost breast high. The Rebs had their slight protection,

but we were in the open, without a thing better than a wheat straw to catch a Minnie bullet that weighed an ounce. Of course, our men began to tumble. They lay where they fell, or, if able, started for the rear. Near to me I saw a man named Daily go down, shot through the neck. I made a movement to get his gun, but at that moment I was struck in the shoulder. It did not hurt and the blow simply caused me to step back. I found that I could not work my arm, but supposed that hurt was a flesh wound that had temporarily paralyzed it, and that it was not serious enough to justify my leaving the fighting line. So, I remained and did what I could in directing the firing. Sometime after this, I felt a blow on the left leg, and it gave way, so that I knew the bone was broken. This stroke did not hurt, and I did not fall, but turned around and made a number of hops to the rear, when my foot caught in the tangled grain and I went down full length. While lying here entirely helpless, and hearing those vicious bullets singing over my head, I suffered from fear. I had, as most men do, got over the dread of battle after I was once fairly in it, and was enjoying the excitement, but when I was "done for" as a fighter, and could only lie in that zone of danger, waiting for other bullets to plow into my body, I confess it was with the greatest dread. While so lying and dreading, in some way, I knew that two men were going to the rear. I yelled out to them, "Drag me back." They heeded the order, or entreaty, and one man grabbed one arm, and the other man the other arm, and they started back with me between them, not on any funeral gait, but almost on a run. My right arm was sound, but the left one was broken at the shoulder joint, and on that side it was pulling on the cords and meat. I wobbled much as a cut of wood drawn by two cords would have. These men pulled me back in this fashion for a number of rods, and until I thought they had pulled me over a rise of ground like a cradle knoll, when I shouted, "Drop me" and they dropped, and went on without note or comment. I had a tourniquet in my haversack, and with my one servicable arm, I worked away till I got it out, and did the best I could to get it around my leg, for anything I knew I was bleeding to death, and, if possible, I wanted to check the flow of blood. I think my effort did not amount to much. After a time the firing tapered down to occasional shots. Of course, I did not know who was on top. Certainly no body of our men had fallen back near my bivouac. In a short time I heard a line of battle advancing from the rear. As the men came in sight I sang out, "Don't step on me, boys!" Those in range of me stepped over and on they went, to take their medicine. I understand they rushed forward and fought the enemy in advance of the line we occupied. It was not many minutes after these troops passed me that the rattle of musketry was again heard from that wheat field. It was kept up for a good while, and then it died down. No body of our men went back past me.

After a while I was aware that a skirmish line was coming from the front, and soon discovered that the skirmishers were not clothed in blue. The officer in command was mounted and rode by within a few feet of me. I should judge that this line went as far as the road I have spoken of. Shots were exchanged at about that distance to the rear of me. This fighting was not severe and a short time after these gentlemen in gray moved back in the same manner they had advanced, greatly to my relief. I did not fancy remaining their guest for any length of time.

As the Rebs went back, a nice looking young fellow, small of stature, with bright black eyes, whose face was smutted up with powder and smoke, came along where I lay. My sword was on the ground beside me. He picked it up, and said, "Give me that scabbard!" I said "Johnny, you will have to excuse me, as my arm is broken and I can't unbuckle my belt." He made no comment, but went off with my sword. Then matters quieted down, and there was no sound to be heard in that vicinity, except the groanings of the wounded. As long as I lay perfectly quiet, I was not in much pain, but if I attempted to stir the pain was severe. I had heard that wounded men always suffered from thirst, but I was not specially thirsty, and I wondered at it. I did not have any desire to groan, and take on, as many about me were doing. So I wondered if I were really badly hurt, and if I could groan, if I wanted to. I determined to try it, and drew in a good breath, and let out a full grown-man groan. I was satisfied with the result and then kept quiet. This action on my part will read like the performance of a simpleton, and I would not record it, but for the fact that it was the freak and experience of one man, helpless on the battlefield. These personal experiences are, of course, less often written about than are the general movements of troops in battle accounts.

After a time I was satisfied our people were establishing a picket line some ways to my rear. I succeeded in securing the attention of a sergeant. He told me the number of his regiment, which was a new Pennsylvania regiment. I told him I wanted to get back out of this debatable belt of land between the skirmish lines. He said he would go and see his officer. In a little while he came back with a Lieutenant, He was a good hearted man, and commiserated my condition, and inquired what he could do for me. I told him my present anxiety was to get to the rear of our skirmish line—that where I then lay was likely to be fought over again, and any little thing would, at least, set the pickets firing at one another. I told him I thought if he and the sergeant would make a chair of their hands, as children often do, they could carry me between them. With difficulty they got me up, and their hands under me, and started, but the broken leg hung down, and caught in the trampled wheat, and I told them I couldn't go it. Then the Lieutenant said he could carry me on his back. I noticed that he had braced up with commissary, and his legs were not wholly reliable, but I thought he could manage me as a pack. So he squatted, and the sergeant helped get me on his back with my arm around his neck. Then he attempted to raise me up, but my weight and the tanglefoot were too much, and we all went down in a heap together, I under. As soon as I could express myself in words, I told the men, if they would straighten me out and cover me up with my blanket, I would excuse them with thanks for their kind intentions. This they did, and left me with no one in sight. It now grew dark rapidly and soon there was as little light as at any time that night. I was wide awake, and my thoughts went on excursions the wide world around.

I think it must have been about midnight—for hours I had heard no sound but the groanings of the men lying on the field about me. All at once I heard a voice. It came from the mouth of Phil Comfort, a private of Co. A. Phil had always been one of the incorrigibles. He would get drunk, and brawl, and fight on the slightest provocation, but he also had the credit of doing much for the wounded of the regiment. I do not know what Phil's business was, out there between the picket lines at midnight of that day. I suspect he may have been there for the purpose of accommodating any corpse that was desirous of being relieved of any valuables he was possessed of, fearing they might be buried in an unmarked grave with his dead body. I never asked Phil about the orders, or from whom they came, that sent him into hailing distance of my place of repose, but I made haste to call Phil up to me. He responded to my call, and in a moment was staring down on me in the starlight. He said, "Why, Lieutenant that's you, aint it!" I admitted the allegation, and said I wanted to get out of here. He replied that he would go for a man and stretcher, and return as soon as possible, and off he went. Before long he was back with man and stretcher, and after much working they got me loaded and started for a point at which the ambulances were assembling. I was set down in the dooryard of a house built of hewed logs, whitewashed. In 1866 I visited the battlefield and this house was standing. I think it has since been removed and a frame house put up on its site.

After an hour's waiting, I was loaded into an ambulance without taking me from my stretcher. This was fortunate for me, as I kept it until it was swaped for a new one two weeks later. The stretcher kept me from the ground, and was an important factor in my recovery. A man was placed beside me shot through the body. He was in an agony of pain, and it was impossible for him to restrain his groans. When the ambulance started, it went anywhere but in a good road, and as it bumped over logs and boulders, my broken leg would thresh about like the mauler of a flail. I found it necessary to keep it in place by putting the other one over it. At last we stopped and were unloaded. It was still dark, but in due time light broke in the East, and a little later I could roll my head and take in some of the surroundings. Most of the wounded of the regiment had been gathered at this place, and we made by far the largest part of it. Many of the men were so hurt that they could move about, and they all came and made me an early morning call. After a time two of our regimental doctors appeared. They cut open my trousers leg, found where the bullet went in, and, I think, put a strip of adhesive plaster over the wound, and they did the same with the shoulder. It was clear to my mind that the leg, at least, must come off. I expressed my opinion and said, I thought it would be better to do it at once, than to wait till inflammation set in. At my earnest request they promised me that they would see to it that I should be among the first operated on.

While in this place my life long friend and companion, Lieut. Isaac Plumb, came to me. We had been side by side since the organization of the regiment, and, until now, neither of us had been badly hurt. He told me that he saw me as I went down, and sang out "Uncle Fuller, that's good for sixty days." He said I made up quite a face, as if it hurt. Shortly afterward he said he had a remarkable experience. He was struck and knocked down, and he supposed a bullet had gone through him, and he was done for. He said he clapped his hands over the place of the supposed wound and held on tight, with the thought that conscious existence might be a little prolonged. He expected to feel life ebbing, but he retained consciousness, and, after a while, lifted his hands, expecting to see an eruption of blood, but he did not. He began to move his body with no bad results, and, finally, got onto his feet, resumed his place and left the field with his men. He did not discover what had happened till he prepared to bunk down for the night, when he unbuckled his sword belt he discovered a strange formation in his vest pocket. In it he had a bunch of small keys on a ring. A Minnie bullet had struck his belt plate square and had glanced so as to go under the plate into his vest pocket, where it met the bunch of keys. There was enough force and resistence to bed the bullet into the ring and the key heads, and there the keys stood out held in place by the embedded bullet. He was able to send this relic of that great battle home, and his mother has it now among her choicest mementos.

After a time the division operating table was set up in the edge of a piece of timber not very far away. I was on the watch, expecting every minute to be taken out, but I waited and waited and no one came for me. I became quite impatient at this delay. I saw one after another brought on, carried up, and taken away, and I was not called for. This aroused my stock of impatience, of which, I naturally always had quiet enough. At last I asked my friend Porter E. Whitney and another man to take me down to the table. I made up my mind, if the mountain did not go to Mahomet, the next best thing was for the prophet to go to the mountain. The men set me down as nearly under the noses of the doctors as could be, and, if something hadn't happened, I presume in a few minutes that heretofore good left leg would have made one of the fast growing pile; but about that interesting moment for me, the enemy began to drop shells that exploded in and about the locality. It was not a fit place to pursue surgical operations. The doctors knew it, so they hastily gathered up their knives and saws, and moved to a place where those projectiles did not drop. The two friends who had taken me there, picked up my stretcher and started for a like place. We had to move several times before the greatest artillery duel of the War began. When that opened we were out of range of it, but we could not hide from the tremble of the ground—the surface of the earth at that place shook and quivered from the terrible concussion of the artillery. The roar was enough to deafen one, and inspire the dread that no one would be left alive and unhurt. Generally however, the noise is a considerable part of such a bombardment. Probably comparatively slight damage was done by it, until our artillery opened on the advancing lines of Pickett's men.

During the day friends occasionally poured water on my wounds, which, doubtless, kept the swelling down.

Pickett was defeated. Grant, Sherman, Sheridan or Thomas, if in command at the time, would have plunged the fresh Sixth Corps on to the rear of Lee's routed men, and effectively crushed him. Meade was new to the place and preferred a respectable certainty to possible disaster. Things quieted down, and that night,

> "Mr. Lee who had come to see
> What he could do about going through,
> The North, turned South."

The boys who were toting me came to a stone house with a wide piazza clear around it. I was laid on the floor of it, which made a hard bed. I ached in every bone, but there was nothing to do but "grin and bear it." After a while Frank Garland of Co. G was brought and laid on the floor near me. He could raise upon his elbow, but his breathing was painful to hear. A bullet had gone through his lungs and every time they filled a portion of the air went through the wound with a ghastly sound. I said to him, "Are you badly wounded, Frank?" He replied, "Oh, yes!"

I had eaten nothing since the morning of the day before, and was faint. Some of our drummer boys found a bin of ground oats, and they made a gruel that tasted good, and I made quite a meal of it. That evening about 10 o'clock, an ambulance came for me, and I was taken to the ground selected for the 2d Corps hospital. It was another rough ride across lots. Once there I was taken out of my stretcher, the one Phil Comfort took me off the field on, and taken at once to the operating table. A napkin was formed into a tunnel shape, a liberal supply of chloroform poured into it and the thing placed over my nose and mouth. I was told to take in long breaths. To me it seemed a long time before the effect came, probably it was a short time, but at last my head seemed to grow big and spin around. At this stage I remember a doctor had his fingers in the wound in the shoulder and said to the others "Here is a fine chance for a resection." I did not know what that meant, but learned afterwards. When I came to myself, I looked down far enough to see a quantity of bandage wound about a stump of a leg eight inches long. My shoulder was bound up, but otherwise not operated on. Failure to resect may have been due to the great amount of work pressing upon the surgeons. They were worked as many hours continuously as they could stand, and still many a man had to be neglected. I was taken off the table and put back on my stretcher, which was set down in a wall tent, this tent was as full as it well could be of amputated cases. For the most part the men bore their suffering without a groan. Among the number was a young Confederate officer, that had lost an arm. He probably felt that he was a good way from home, and he "took on," bemoaning his fate as a cripple and a sufferer. He wore out the patience of every other man in the tent. At last I yelled out to him to shut up, or I would get up and kick him out doors. My bark was effective, we heard no more from him. All of us were amputates, or seriously wounded. During the night a doctor came, and gave every man a dose of morphine, which produced a happy state of mind and body. As I was taken from the table one of my doctors said, "Fuller, you may drink all of the whiskey you can get, and want."

The day of the 4th we had a drenching rain. Some men out lying in low places and who could not move were, it was said, drowned. On the whole, I presume the rain was a benefit to the wounded.

It took a number of days for the large hospital tents to be put up. All of the sound part of the army that could be spared followed up the enemy. Of course, it took a large number of soldiers detailed for the purpose, to partially care for the thousands of wounded from each army. The surgeons were continuously engaged upon new cases that had received no attention. Those of us that had been treated knew this, and we found no fault at what otherwise would have been terrible neglect. I think it was six days after my amputation before a doctor could be found to look at my stump. The night before I had been made very nervous by crawley feelings on that side of me, just where I could not tell. It is, I think, the rule with amputations, that the patient cannot from the feeling put his hand on the place of amputation. It takes a good while for the nerves to realize where "the end" is. They were made to carry the news to the brain from the extremities, and, until the new arrangement has become somewhat acquainted with the change, these lines of communication are doing duty for parts of the body not there. My bad feelings were not at the end of the stump, but down in the foot and ankle, where there were constant beats, and pulls and cramps. I think this is the foundation for the many fairy stories to the effect that an amputated leg or arm buried gave the owner of it great pain, as if something pressed on it, or it was cramped in its box, and when it was opened up there was found a stone between the fingers, or the cover jammed upon the foot, and that when the cause of discomfort was removed then the stump of the arm or leg was easy. As in the various phases of faith cure, the imagination has a powerful effect. So it has in these cases. It is never that there is a real feeling connected between the severed part and the body, but the belief in it creates a supposed reality.

It was the good fortune of our tent that a civilian surgeon from Ohio visiting the field came along and offered his services to any of us that wanted him to do for us. I told him how I had felt through the night, and I would be glad to have him dress my stump. He took the bandages off and found that there were a large number of full grown maggots in the wound. This discovery for the moment was horrifying to me. I concluded if all the other things did not take me off the skippers would, but the good doctor assured me that the wigglers didn't amount to much in that place, and he would soon fix them. He diluted some turpentine, took a quantity of it in his mouth and squirted it into the wound, and over the stump. It did the business for the intruders, and I had no more trouble of that sort.

The morning of the 4th of July Capt. Keech came to me and said he was to have a short leave of absence on account of the wound he received in the neck, which came near effectually cutting it. He wanted to know what word he should convey to my people. I said tell them I am doing as well as one can under the circumstance. He replied, "Don't you want them to come down here?" I said, "No!" "They can do no good here, and will be in the way." When he got to New York he wired to Sherburne: "Garland mortally wounded. Fuller dangerously wounded. Plumb all right."

That night my father started for Unadilla Forks to see Dr. King, his brother-in-law. The doctor was one of the best surgeons in Otsego Co. My father told him he wanted him to go to Gettysburg and look after me. They were in Utica the next morning ready for the first train East. From a newsboy they got a *Herald*, which gave a long list of New York casualties. Finally they struck '' Lieut. C. A. Fuller, Co. C. 61st N. Y., leg *and arm amputated.*'' The doctor said, '' If that is true there is not much chance for Charley, but we will go on and bring him home alive or dead.'' And so they went on.

All this is very tame and personal, and, in many ways, I know can be of but small interest. There is this to be said of it: It shows what was going on in thousands of families the land over —North and South—and it is the kind of matter that does not get into books on war subjects. The reality of war is largely obscured by descriptions that tell of movements and maneuvers of armies, of the attack and repulse, of the victory and defeat, and then pass on to new operations. All of this leaves out of sight the fellows stretched out with holes through them, or with legs and arms off.

At Baltimore my father had to turn back on account of acute illness. From New York my father and Uncle were accompanied by my cousin Edward Snyder. He was a grand man. He had tried several times to enter the service, but was rejected. For years he had been in the employ of the American Express Co. and knew how to push his way through a crowd. The jam was so great to get to the battlefield, and the transportation so inadequate, they might have been delayed several days, but for the steering qualifications of Snyder. He elbowed and managed in such a way that he and the doctor got onto an open flat bottomed car headed for Gettysburg the same day. On their arrival it was no small job to find me, but a half day's search and inquiry brought them to my tent, a large hospital tent holding some sixteen men, everyone of whom had, I believed, sustained an amputation. They had found the Chaplain of the 64th New York, a thoroughly good man, qualified for the office, as many chaplains were not. This Chaplain had been of great service since the battle ; his work in behalf of the men was tireless. Earlier in the day he had talked with me, trying to brace me up and make me hopeful. I remember saying to him, "If I were where I could have the best of care; I might pull through, but that is impossible." I knew that my chances were few and scant. About noon he came to me and said, "Fuller, can you stand some good news?" I said, "Yes, if ever I could I can now." He said, "Some one has come to see you?" I asked, "Is it Dr. King?" He said, "Yes." I looked to the other side of the tent, and there in the doorway stood my uncle, and just behind him Edward Snyder. The doctor was short and thick and Snyder was tall and thin, so I had a view of both of their faces at once. It was a sight so photographed in my memory that it is as fresh to-day as when it was taken. The doctor remained at the field hospital for about ten days. During that time he took charge of about a dozen amputated cases, and while he was rather squatty for an Angel, the men regarded him as one of mercy. By the end of ten days from his coming the doctor told me that I was making no progress and ought to be moved where I could get better air. He got permission for my removal into the village. Two men carried me on a stretcher. When the doctor left the boys he had been caring for, there were few dry eyes on their faces. I was taken to the house of Mr. Carson, cashier of one of the banks. On the approach of Lee's army, Mr. Carson had taken the cash and valuables to Philadelphia. At this time every house in town was at the service of any wounded, or their friends. When I was deposited at his house, Mr. Carson was in Philadelphia to get and return the bank's property, but Mrs. Carson was there, and, if I had been a near relative, she could not have done more to make my stay tolerable. As an instance of the romance in war the following occurred. Mrs. Carson's brother was an officer in a Maine battery. He was in the first day's engagement and was quite badly wounded. He managed to get to his sister's house, I believe he was not disturbed by the Rebels, and left for his home the day before I came.

After a few days in the village, consent was obtained for me to start for home. We were on the way for about a week, and everywhere on the route the greatest kindness was shown save in one instance. That was at the Albany station, and with the New York Central's employees. It was necessary to put my stretcher with me on it into the baggage car. I was set down by the side of the car, asking that it be done. By the treatment I got from the men in charge, one would take them to be a gang of copperheads. Seeing that they were going to refuse me admission to the car, I began to call them off in no gentle manner. My billingsgate caused a crowd to gather. I informed the trainmen and the people assembled that if I could have a squad of my regiment there for a very few minutes, I would go in that car, or that train would be a wreck. I soon had the sympathy of the lookers on, and some of them suggested that I would go into that car, or it might not be necessary for me to have any of the 61st there to make things interesting. The disobliging servants of the road did not care to have more of a demonstration, and the door was shoved open, and, in no gracious manner, I was put on board, and started for Utica. I think those New York Central loafers would have left me there to have fly-blowed had they not feared the temper of the crowd. It was a painful surprise to me to meet such indifference, if not hostility, in Central New York, when I had just experienced such helpful kindness in Baltimore, Philadelphia, and even in New York, a place that usually cares for nothing and no one, except commercially. From Utica I was taken in an ambulance to Unadilla Forks, N. Y.

At the end of a week my shoulder was operated on, and three inches of the humerus taken out from the shoulder joint down. The operation was performed by Dr. King, and was an excellent one. A week after that operation, an incision was made into the stump and the bullet that broke the leg was taken out. That it was in the stump was, of course, a surprise, and when the surgeons of my regiment were informed what had been done, they claimed to be much surprised, and said that they traced out the bullet that they amputated for, and that the bullet extracted by Dr. King must have been a second one. I have always had the impression that I was hit in the leg lower down, and before the one came that broke the leg, but of that I am not certain.

With two such wounds as I had, and one poisoned for six

weeks with a Minnie bullet, it was a slow process to recover, but I made steady progress with, of course, occasional pull backs.

I think it was in September, 1863, and after I reached my home, that George Jacobs, a sergeant in my company of New Berlin, called on me. George was *one* of the best soldiers in the regiment. In a fight no one could be better. He was home on a ten days furlough. Of course, the best in the land was free to him, and he was feasted by parents and friends. As he was about ready to start back, he was taken violently sick with a stomach trouble and died in a few hours.

In December, 1863, I was ordered to report at a hospital at Annapolis, Md. I started alone with one crutch, and my arm in a sling. At Albany I stopped over night with my cousin Stewart Campbell, and well remember that evening reading in the *Atlantic Monthly* that wonderful story, " A Man Without a Country," by Edward Everett Hale. It made a deep impression on my mind and it confirmed the sentiment I had cherished that it was well worth hardship, wounds, loss of limbs, or life even, to have a hand in preserving in its integrity such a country as ours. I reached Anapolis all right. In about a week I was ordered to Washington, and mustered out. This ended my connection with one of the best regiments in the service in the War of the Rebellion. I do not say this, I think, unadvisedly, nor from a mistaken sense of the quality of the rank and file of the regiment, but rather from the character of the commanding officers of the regiment while under Barlow and Miles. Each of them officers whose equal it was hard to find. They were men of dauntless courage and rare military judgment, who LED their men into battle, and under them if a soldier wanted to slink, as a rule, he deemed it safer to face the enemy than to let either one of them suspect he was slinking.

I have now told my story as a soldier, and the purpose of this pamphlet is ended. In conclusion I want to register my admiration for the war power of a country. It is a splendid employment to be in the Army, or Navy of one's country! The office of the War Power is to maintain order and right at home, and defend the flag from foreign aggression. It is not the first and main business of the soldier to kill anyone ; he is put in motion only after peacable means for righteousness have failed. Then he comes forward and says to the obstructor and the enemy of right: "Desist, surrender, give way !" and it is only after refusal and a show of hostile force that the soldier shoots his gun, and when he shoots he prefers to wound, disable and capture, rather than to kill.

Of course, we all ought to encourage the avoidance of war, and the promotion of peace, but the wise ruler, while so doing, will have an adequate army to make it certain that he cannot be overborne by evil-minded persons, and the enemies of his government. Mankind must be dealt with as it is, and not on a fanciful, theoretical basis.

Really the Army is the strong arm of the executive part of the governmental machinery. The sheriff and constable may be resisted and fail ; the posse comitatus they call to their aid may prove inadequate, and then there is nothing to look to but the Army.

If I had a son 18 years of age, I would not feel bad to see him enrolled for a three years enlistment in the United States Army, or Navy. I would expect he would be discharged at the end of the term improved by the discipline. The wearer of the uniform ought to be honored by the people and accorded as broad a place in society as if he were a member of what is termed " one of the learned professions." The treatment accorded our soldiers and sailors by some rich, ill-bred snobs in this country is to their lasting disgrace, and it is to be hoped that such stupid idiots may live to see the day when they will bitterly repent their fool actions.

After Gettysburg

Life is real! Life is earnest!
And the grave is not its goal;
Dust thou art, to dust returnest,
Was not spoken of the soul.

Henry Wadsworth Longfellow

For Charles Fuller there was life after Gettysburg, 53 years of it, and it was those years that mark him as an extraordinary man. His wartime experiences were shared by countless other men, North and South, but not many as permanently handicapped as he would recover so quickly to go on to live a full and meaningful life. A small man, 5'6" and 135 pounds, he lost none of his spirit and his zeal for life.

His skirmish with death, unlike the leg which remained in an unmarked grave on the field, could not be forgotten. Forty-three years later he wrote of a recent visit to the 61st New York Monument in the Wheatfield: "As I stood in front of this monument commemorating the deeds of the 61st NY on that day, standing there alone in that field, I took my hat off reverently and expressed my thanks for the preservation extended to me in those hours, and endeavored to commune with my comrades who there passed out from their toil and endeavor as soldiers, and who there gave up their lives in a brave effort to defeat the enemy of their Government. . . . I was glad no one was about to distract my attention or talk the matter over. It was peculiarly a place for solitude and silence, and I am today thankful that I had the privilege to stand there, and as far as possible, live over the hours of that important day in my own life."

The haunting memories of lost friends made every day a memorial day for him. Especially grievous for him was the loss of his life-long friend Isaac Plumb, mortally wounded on the picket line three days after the futile Union assault at Cold Harbor. Fuller collected and preserved Plumb's wartime letters to his family.

Rather than lament his ill fortune, Fuller chose to view his survival and recovery as good fortune provided by Providence, something for which to be thankful. He had been given a life not to be wasted in idle self-pity or heroic posturing. His positive and optimistic attitude may well have contributed to his recovery and return to active life.

The timely arrival of his uncle, Dr. King, at Gettysburg and his subsequent operations to remove minie balls from Charles's shoulder, and from what the nephew later referred to as "a small apology for a leg," were important factors contributing to his recovery. Nevertheless, that recovery and return to civilian life were accomplished without benefit of a Veterans Hospital, physical therapy or psychological counseling. And artificial limbs were accurately described as "wooden legs."

Six months after Gettysburg, Fuller travelled alone by train to Annapolis and Washington to be discharged, hopping on his right leg with the help of a crutch held by his right arm, his left arm in a sling. The head of the humerus that joined his left arm to his shoulder joint had been shattered and was removed by Dr. King. Fuller was left with a "disconnected" arm. Unable to raise itself, it hung limply at his side supported by what Fuller termed as "cords and meat."

Walking with a cane and an artificial limb, Fuller attended Albany Law School in 1864-65 and was admitted to the bar in 1865. He practiced for a year in Hamilton, New York before returning to Sherburne in 1866 to open the law offices he was to occupy for 50 years.

Fuller chose to live out the remainder of his life in Sherburne, a small crossroads village in south central upstate New York that served as a trading center for farmers from the surrounding rural area. Both his maternal and paternal grandparents were Connecticut families who had immigrated to the area shortly after the Revolution, while it was still a frontier wilderness. Prior to the Revolution this region, with its eastern boundary marked by the Unadilla River, some 10 miles west of Sherburne, had been part of the Iroquois Nation, as provided by the 1768 Ft. Stanwix Treaty between England and the five Iroquois tribes. A second treaty, after the war between New York and the Iroquois, opened the area to white settlers, many of them veterans of the Continental Army, and most of them from New England.

The grandparents, Elijah and Ruth Robinson Fuller, and Gideon (a veteran of the Revolution) and Hannah DeForest settled within a few miles of each other, cleared the forest, built their homesteads and settled down to till the soil along the Unadilla. Thomas A. Fuller, Charles's father, married Harriet DeForest on August 21, 1840.

Six months after the birth of Charles, on August 17, 1841, in the Chenango County Town of Columbus, the family moved to Sherburne. Thomas Fuller had prospered working his father's farm and at 30 was able to purchase a general merchandise store in Sherburne, a brick block whose second floor offices would later house his son's law office. The elder Fuller also acquired a handsome brick house on East State Street, a block east of the store. Both properties were later willed to Charles following his father's death in 1875. His mother, Harriet DeForest Fuller, lived in the house until her death in 1899.

The parents, if not wealthy, were well-to-do by small town mid-19th century standards. Their good fortune allowed Charles, after attending Sherburne schools, to attend two terms in 1860-61 at Madison University, now Colgate University, in Hamilton. The War found Charles in Cleveland, Ohio, where he had entered upon the legal career that he was able to continue after 1863.

On June 23, 1869 Charles, then 27, and Mary E. Matthewson, 24, daughter of Albert T. and Mary Blair Matthewson of Norwich, were married in the Norwich Baptist Church, entering upon a union that was to last for 47 years. Mary bore him three daughters, Addie Louise, born September 9, 1870, Mary Antoinette, "Little Nettie," born August 21, 1873, and Mary DeForest, born May 10, 1882.

For almost a lifetime Mary gave her moral and physical support to a man whom some Victorian brides must have considered to be physically "blemished," and in the parlance of the day, "crippled." Mary proved to be a good judge of character. She died in 1919 and is buried in the Sherburne Quarter Cemetery with Charles and "Little Nettie."

As if his War experience were not enough to test his resiliency, Fuller was not spared the anguish of family tragedy. His second child, "Little Nettie," the namesake of his only sister, who herself had died in 1862 at the age of 12, died before her third birthday. The other daughters, however, married and reared families.

Addie Louise married Charles L. Carrier and had two children, Rush and Harriet Carrier West. Harriet had no children, but Rush had two sons, Charles L. and Thomas, both living. Charles L. has four sons, one named Charles Fuller Carrier. Dr. Thomas Carrier has three daughters.

Marion married Ward N. Truesdall, who in 1906 had become her father's law partner. Two sons, Robert F. and Charles W. were born to this marriage. Robert died in early manhood, but the second grandson, Charles W. Truesdall, is living and has three daughters and a son.

One grandson, six great grandchildren and seven great, great grandchildren, all living, can proudly claim to be descendants of Charles and Mary Fuller.[1]

Fuller became a familiar figure to Sherburne residents as he went about his daily business for 50 years, doing what he later described as "work of various kinds." Miss Agnes Casey, now 95 and a high school student at the time, remembers him as being "civic minded," "a kind and friendly man," and she recalls that he "moved right along," scarcely slowed by his disability.

A practicing lawyer, he served as Village Postmaster from 1867-87. He was active in state and local politics, an ardent Republican, and, in 1888, was elected to the State Legislature and later to the 1894 New York State Constitutional Convention. Fuller served several terms as Village Trustee and Village President, was a member and President of the Board of Education for many years, and addressed the students and teachers each fall at the opening of the school year. He was a member of

[1]Mrs. Rush Carrier, Hamilton, NY, provided the information regarding the Fuller descendants. Dates were obtained from "The Genealogical and Family History of Central New York," edited by William Richard Cutter, New York: Lewis Historical Publishing Co., 1912 and the Fuller gravestone in the Sherburne Quarter Cemetery.

the Village Library Board until his death, organized the Women's Village Improvement Society, served as Justice of the Peace, and was a faithful member of the Sherburne Congregational Church. He played an active role in Memorial Day services and in the affairs of the Sherburne Isaac A. Plumb GAR Post, and had even donated the village flag which hung at half-mast on the day of his funeral. His obituary noted that: "Mr. Fuller was actively interested in the best things for the Community. He was ready to support every good cause according to his ability and means."

In the fall of 1906, then 65, he wrote a detailed account of his recovery and return to Sherburne after Gettysburg in a series of letters to the *Sherburne News* entitled "Forty-three Years Later." He concluded the last letter: "I got well and since have done no small amount of work of various kinds, and for a fact, while no person can accurately number his days, I feel as if I have quite a store of activity left, and I hope for sometime to come, speaking nautically and figuratively, to be on deck and take my trick at the wheel."

These were the prophetic words of a man who earned considerable honor in his home town and among his kin, and who was remembered as "highly respected," "a patriot," "good citizen, neighbor and friend." It was the highest tribute a small town could pay to one of its own.

On July 1, 1889 he had returned to the Wheatfield to give the principal address at the dedication of the 61st New York Monument. He summed up the hope and purpose that marked his life: "Our patriotism is brightened, our regard for the land we fought for is enhanced, and we will return to our homes better fitted to the remnant of our work, part of which is to perfect the Government we saved."

Fuller shared the patriotism of his Victorian peers, and never doubted that the War was a just and necessary one. Like many others of his generation he believed that the world was becoming a better place in which to live, but harbored no illusions about the human nature that constantly threatened that progress. He wrote: "Mankind must be dealt with as it is, and not on a fanciful, theoretical basis." He did not believe in moral evolution. His hope and optimism were born of a strong religious faith that had been tested in the Chickahominy Swamp, the Sunken Lane at Antietam, at Marye's Heights, in the Chancellorsville Wilderness and in the Wheatfield.

His gravestone reads simply, but proudly:

Charles A. Fuller
Co. C 61st N.Y.S. Inf.
Born—August 17, 1841
Died—October 27, 1916

Norwich, NY   Herb S. Crumb
January 1990

2nd Lt. Charles A. Fuller, Co. C, 61st Regt. NYS Vol. Inf. (Courtesy of the Division of Military and Naval Affairs NYS Adjt. Gen. Office, Albany, NY)

Officers of the 61st NY Inf., Falmouth, VA, 1863. Front Row: 1st Lt. George B. Elmore, Capt. Nathan C. Bull, Capt. Edward C. Kittle, Capt. Willard Keech, 1st Lt. Rufus L. Rundell, 1st Lt. George W. Wren. Middle Row: Capt. Lee Nutting, Asst. Surgeon William P. Bush, Chaplain H. D. Burdock, Capt. Henry C. Williams. Back Row: Capt. Isaac Plumb, 2nd Lt. Charles A. Fuller, Capt. Cornelius P. Bergen, 1st Lt. Frank W. Grannis, Col. George W. Scott, Col. Nelson A. Miles, Lt. Col. Oscar K. Broady, Capt. Peter C. Bain, 1st Lt. James A. Owens, Capt. Thomas G. Morrison. (Courtesy of the Massachusetts Commandery Military Order of the Loyal Legion and the US Army Military History Institute)

Sixty-first New York Infantry Regimental Monument in the Wheatfield, Gettysburg, PA.

The Fuller Home, Sherburne, New York.

Index

Personal Recollections of the War of 1861

ERRATA

Page 111, insert "Marion" in place of "Mary" (DeForest) in line 8 from the bottom.

Page 112, insert "Truesdell" in place of "Truesdall" in lines 12 and 15 from the top.